The Heart of a Ninja
for Kids

It's Play Time!

Live Like a Ninja

Also by Chris Warnky

The Heart of a Ninja: Stretch Your Boundaries

What Just Happened?: The Line

What Just Happened?: The Run

 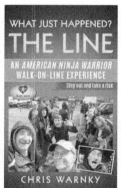 

The Heart of a Ninja for Kids

It's play time!

Chris Warnky

Well Done Life LLC

Columbus, Ohio

2019

Well Done
Life

Chris Warnky/Well Done Life LLC
1440 Mentor Drive
Westerville, Ohio 43081

Editor: Gwen Hoffnagle
Cover Layout by Fiverr pro_ebookcovers
Book Layout © 2017 BookDesignTemplates.com

Ordering Information:
Quantity sales: Special discounts are available on quantity purchases by corporations, associations, and others. For details contact "Special Sales" at the above address.

The Heart of a Ninja for Kids: It's Play Time! / Chris Warnky – 1st ed.
ISBN 978-0-9993331-5-0

Dedication

This book is dedicated to our Creator/God. He has allowed me to live a very blessed life.

It's also dedicated to the great young and aspiring ninjas who are training and dreaming of one day getting to compete on *American Ninja Warrior*.

Contents

Introduction

I wrote *The Heart of a Ninja for Kids* to encourage you to get out and move and play in this ninja world playground that I've found to be so fun. I hope through sharing my experiences, stories, and example you will be encouraged to be more active. I have a dream that thousands of kids will physically move and play more, which will improve their lives.

Is this Chris Warnky, the author of the book *The Heart of a Ninja*?

A couple of years ago I was sitting at a Panera Bread evaluating the coaching session I had just conducted. As I sat there, about to take a drink, my phone rang. I looked at my phone and saw that it was a New York phone number and I didn't know the caller. I decided to let it go. I was guessing it was some type of sales call. I went back to my assessment for a minute longer and the call came in again. This time I decided to take the call and tell them not to call me anymore. I answered the phone and said, "Chris Warnky speaking." What sounded like the voice of a young boy said, "Is this Chris Warnky, the author of *The Heart of a Ninja*?" I replied, "Yes it is." He shared with me how excited he was to get to talk personally to the author of the book and the dad of popular ninja Michelle Warnky. He said he had really enjoyed the book, and we spoke for a few minutes. I could hear his mom in the background, and just before we ended our conversation she asked if she could talk with me.

This is how I became Rafi Ellison's mentor. He is a tremendous fan of *American Ninja Warrior* (*ANW*) and has grown into an unbelievably strong ninja, now in his early teens. It has been great to work with him over this period, to enjoy  our ninja talk, and also to talk about life skills and the 12 traits of a ninja. He made some great choices during this time, and I loved the opportunity to build a relationship with him and watch him grow.

I've heard from other parents across the U.S. about how much their kids loved reading *The Heart of a Ninja*, which was primarily written for adults in their 40s and older. So I decided to modify and shorten the original book and target it to relate even better to kids. *The Heart of a Ninja for Kids* was born.

American Ninja Warrior Junior®

Since the original version of *The Heart of a Ninja* a whole new level of competition has surfaced on the national and TV level: *ANW Junior*. Through this show young kids have the opportunity to compete on an official *ANW* course. The popularity of the shows and the sport continues to increase and many kids and adults are reaping the benefits from the entertainment, exercise, relationships, and experiences. *The Heart of a Ninja for Kids* adds to this amazing ninja experience.

I Won and Gained the Heart of a Ninja

I developed the heart of a ninja over the last five years. I feel even younger than I did when I started at age 57. I have won in the way that I've lived my life, spending significant time in ninja activities:

moving, playing, gaining strength and balance, and learning and growing as a person. I'm excited about taking you along as I retrace my first few years as a ninja. It has been such a great ride, creating an even better future for me. I'm fully convinced that you can experience the same.

ANW boldly moved into my life and made me a better person. I hope you will enjoy this ride as much as I have.

There is so much I would love to share that I think you will enjoy and that will be interesting and helpful. *The Heart of a Ninja for Kids* was written for those who love *ANW*, those who want to become a ninja or are starting their ninja journey, and those who are curious about behind-the-scenes ninja activities. It's especially for those who have said, either in your mind or maybe even out loud, "I could do that!" or even, "Wow, I could never do anything like that!" I share many insights about my training experience that I hope you will find interesting and motivating.

Play

Play is when we get creative or set up a game-like environment in which we strive to win. It might be trying to beat our prior best performance in an activity, like doing it better or faster. Play includes the excitement and anticipation of

success or failure, and the thrill of pushing ourselves as far as we can, like running as hard as we can, zigging and zagging to tag someone in a game of tag, or maybe doing our best to avoid being tagged. It's a fun yet safe environment in which it doesn't matter whether we win or lose. Play is a very fun and healthy aspect of life. We don't have to play all the time, but we can benefit from playing often.

Dipping Your Toe In

How close have you come to dipping your toe in the ninja warrior waters? Have you tried a ninja obstacle or a full course run rather than just cheering on those fantastic competitors from the sideline or from your couch? I hope my story will inspire you to give it a try. When you do, I guarantee you will have more fun, experience encouragement, gain strength, and have more friends than you can possibly imagine. You might come away with some aches, pains, a few injuries, and some disappointments, but you won't want to trade them for the world for the positive impacts ninja play will have on your life.

I hope to provide you with:

- A fun ride as I take you along on my journey so you can see, hear, feel, and touch my ninja experience
- Encouragement and hope for more fun and better health
- An example to follow
- Ideas to consider

The Heart of a Ninja for Kids has three primary sections. The first part is about my personal ninja experiences. Next I share 12 traits of a ninja. Then you will read some insights from other ninjas who have competed on *ANW*. At the end I provide information that might be helpful if you want to train as a ninja.

Bitten and Hooked

I'm convinced that as you read you will get hooked and want more. The next thing you know, you will be laughing more with new and exciting friends. You will look in the mirror one of these days and notice that you look dif-ferent. It might be because of your increased strength, your improved balance, or your greater confidence in who you are. It might be due to what you can now do and who you are becoming. This is such a powerful experience. I hope you get hooked!

Ninja Kids

Throughout this book I include photos of ninja kids I know through either Movement Lab Ohio (MLAB OH), my daughter's gym in Columbus, Ohio, where I train and teach, or through ninjas I featured in the original *The Heart of a Ninja* book. You will see photos of the following ninjas:

Dylan Yee

Noah Buschur

Rafi Ellison

Sydney Yee

Free Gifts!

If you would like to receive any of the following free gifts, please request them at chriswarnky@gmail.com.

- A short video greeting from me with a bonus ninja training experience story

- A bonus story about my 2017 National Ninja League announcing experience

Let's dive into the Chris Warnky ninja experience and see how it can encourage and inspire you to have more fun and live an even better life.

My Ninja Experience

Becoming a Ninja

Just a few years ago, I had never heard of *ANW*. If it had come up in a conversation I probably wouldn't even have paid attention. *Sasuke*, which is the original version of ninja warrior, was a big deal in Japan and had been for years, and *ANW* had already made a big splash in the United States on the G4 television network. I was introduced to *ANW* by my daughter, Michelle, and my wife, Carolyn, in 2012, during season four of *ANW*.

Ninja Warrior Has Taken Over

Today, in many ways, ninja warrior has taken over much of my life. Some families get so absorbed about March Madness, which occurs during the end of the college basketball season, and that's all

they talk about during that intense three-week period. At our home the conversation includes talk about Michelle's performance at an *ANW* city qualifier; we talk about things going on at Michelle's ninja gym; we talk about the latest ninja obstacle I would like to hang or set up in our garage or basement; we talk about where we'll stay when we go and cheer on the competitors at the National Ninja League (NNL) finals – I could go on and on. We are a family who talks a lot about *ANW*.

Over 40 All-Nighters

Now I know about *ANW*. I've spent over 40 all-nighters, or all-dayers, at ninja competition sites. I know hundreds of ninjas who have competed on the show. I've personally spent well over 1,000 hours training on ninja obstacles and competing on courses. I'm very familiar with this addictive new sport. It's a lot of fun to watch and even more fun to do.

How many ninjas do you know by name, by sight, or by their story? Some of you even know how many seasons some of the ninjas have competed and how far they have gone. It's easy to get sucked in and it's a lot of fun to follow and even more fun to train. I'm guessing you know about this level of intense and sometimes obsessive *ANW* conversation, and you can relate to how much fun it is and how consuming it can be.

What is the primary topic of conversation at your home? How absorbed are you in *ANW*?

When Did My Ninja Journey Begin?

I remember back to my fourth-grade class at Mount Pleasant Grade School in St. Louis, Missouri. The bell rings and it's recess time. Yay! It's one of those recesses when I'm not staying inside to write sentences because I was talking in class. It's a warm and sunny day and I get to play on the playground, the monkey bars, or what we called the jungle gym. It's so much fun to climb across it, walk on top of it, and swing from bar to bar. The eight long, gray metal pipes are much larger than my hands, and I make my way across the horizontal ladder with only my hands, trying to see how many I can skip without falling.

Speaking of falling, it would have been a five- or six-foot drop to the asphalt. I had several of those experiences that resulted in a badly skinned knee or elbow, or at minimum a fresh, red-colored scrape, or in the worst cases some blood running down my arm or leg. Those

were the days! As Tarzan, a monkey, or a trapeze artist, I did my best to fly through the air. It was anything but boring. The freedom I felt and the fun I experienced on those

bars are great memories.

How about you? Do you have a special place like this where you can be creative and do both risky and fun things, pushing yourself to see how far you can go? I hope you do. It was a good time with a lot of enjoyment and creativity.

Our Kids

To a much lesser degree I experienced some of this fun again with my two kids, Tim and Michelle, as they were growing up. We played various games, running somewhere or jumping to or from something. We would see who could jump the farthest down the sidewalk, or whatever it might be. We loved seeing who could go the farthest or the fastest, always striving to beat our records.

As a Grown-Up

Now that I'm in my 60s, I've found a way to get back to the same type of feeling I had when I was in grade school. Have you found a way to be creative, push yourself, and set new milestones in jumping, running, swinging, and rolling? I've found that when I move in this way I get a fantastic workout that is very good for my health. This is especially true as I continue to get older, or more mature.

Today I'm a ninja. This is what takes me back to those fun early days. If I can be a ninja, you can too. To me, a ninja is anyone who enjoys moving in ways that involves climbing, jumping, swinging, or hanging on objects. All we need is the right attitude and to learn how to use our amazing bodies and minds. Anyone can become a ninja. I believe there is a ninja inside each of us, ready to wake up and come out and play. We all fall somewhere on the ninja spectrum, ranging from amateurs to top performers on *ANW*. Even at the top level there is a wide range of skills and abilities.

An Athlete?

Many ninjas I train with were athletes in their younger days. One day at an MLAB OH open gym, my fellow ninjas were warming up and sharing their athletic backgrounds. Shanon Paglieri had been a gymnast in high school; Scott Walberry played varsity baseball in high school and in college; Katie Tennant had been a wrestler in high school, competing on the boys' team, and was currently a high school track coach; and Sean Noel had been a wrestler in high school. Ninja gyms and the ninja sport draw all types of athletes. It's a fun way to get to continue to work out and play.

Then you have your non-athlete: someone who has always loved sports and played in their neighborhoods but was never on a formal team in school and never had a coach to help them develop their physical skills and abilities. That is me. I'm the non-athlete of the group. Yet I'm loved, welcomed, and supported as much as every other ninja in the gym. I'm treated just like everyone else. (Later I will share much more about the fantastic ninja community I've come to know and love.) I'm the non-athlete who is having a ball playing on the playground again, just as I did over 50 years ago. It's every bit as much fun and probably even better for me than it was back then.

Making the Decision to Ninja Train

My ninja quest started over five years ago after my wife, Carolyn, and my daughter, Michelle, started watching *ANW*. Michelle had been teaching English in Kazakhstan during the school year for five years. She returned to the U.S. in 2011. Three of her friends who were familiar with *ANW* reached out to her and asked, "Have you seen this show? You'll love it!" Michelle watched the show and came away excited, wanting to find out how to compete on it. Carolyn and Michelle got into watching *ANW 4,* a season before I paid much attention. Soon Michelle looked into how she could get to a ninja gym so she could find out how she would do on the obstacles. She really wanted to play on them.

And most ninjas do consider it playing when they're on the ninja obstacles. It's a chance to play, test your skills, and see how far you can go. Michelle made a few trips to ninja gyms, the first one was to Movement Lab New Jersey, the gym owned by *ANW* veteran Chris Wilczewski and his brother Brian. She fell in love with the people, the obstacles, and ninja warrior. Chris was impressed with her ability on the salmon ladder, stating, "I've never seen a woman beat the salmon ladder before." Michelle was hooked.

Eventually she was contacted by the folks at *ANW*. They said they had heard she had built some obstacles and they encouraged her to submit an application and create a submission video to be considered for the show. She did, and they invited her to compete on *ANW 5* that year.

Both Carolyn and I have been Michelle's biggest fans for her track and cross-country competitions since she was in middle school. We got very involved as fans and supporters when she competed in *ANW*. The ninja environment and people are addicting. They are so much fun to be around.

What If?

"What if?" is one of the questions I ask my coaching clients when they're talking about their potential, their desires and goals, and their options. This is a powerful question that opens new doors that can lead to many new options and experiences for my clients. It was now my turn to ask myself, "What if?"

By mid-2014, after Michelle was one of the first three women to reach the top of the warped wall in a qualifier competition, I started to think about what it would be like to play on the obstacles myself, at a gym or maybe even on the NBC *ANW* course. The more I thought about it, the more I liked the idea of getting involved. It also really scared me when I thought about doing those things that Paul Kasemir, Andrew Karsen, Elet Hall, Ryan Stratis, and Drew Drechsel were doing. It was stimulating, and yet a very scary thought.

I was a 57-year-old non-athlete who was inactive other than walking on a treadmill for 45 minutes, six days a week. I hadn't even begun walking on the treadmill until the year 2000, when I started exercising for the first time in nearly 20 years. I didn't even run on the treadmill; I walked at a generally fast pace.

As we moved into July of 2014, the idea hit me, "What if Michelle and I could be the first daughter and dad to compete on the show?" There had already been dads and sons, brothers, sisters, a brother and a sister, and many other family combinations, but no daughter and dad. And there was no fan-favorite "Michelle Warnky" and dad. At that time Michelle was a two-time *ANW* "Las Vegas Finals" contestant.

After letting that idea settle in my mind for a few weeks, I mentioned it to Michelle. There was a part of me that was shaking in my boots about mentioning it to anyone, especially Michelle. What if she didn't like the idea, or if she really liked the idea, and all of a sudden I would be facing some major expectations? Was I ready for this? I didn't know.

Michelle was excited about the possibility and said, "Dad, you should do it. You should do it!" With a grin on my face and my eyes starting to roll into my head, I was wondering what I was doing. I thought, "Can I really commit to doing this?" I eventually said I would. I told her I would probably need 18 to 24 months to train to be a reasonably serious competitor. She agreed, and has supported me through my entire journey. I trained for 18 months, completed an *ANW* application, and created a submission video for the 2016 season of *ANW*.

Below are the links to two of my YouTube *ANW* submission videos.

2016 *ANW 8*:

https://www.youtube.com/watch?v=id5XlRs85QY&t=5s

2017 *ANW 9*:

https://www.youtube.com/watch?v=WPpOy_ju_Xo&t=1s

Where My Journey Has Taken Me

My journey has taken me from my fun days back in grade school, to many stagnant years as an adult, and then to the present day, when I'm again having that same fun on a ninja playground. I feel like I win every time I step into a ninja gym to play again. The feeling I get inside is the same; it's just a little different playground and I have a little older body – by 50 years.

What would a win like that look like for you?

What would it feel like to have more fun, be in better shape, and develop the heart of a ninja?

What is it like to sit and wait to find out if you have been invited to compete on *ANW*? It can be really hard! I share my experience with you in the next chapter.

I Win during *ANW 8*!

I sat on pins and needles for three weeks while I waited for "the call." When would the calls begin? They normally started three to five weeks before the competitions, and it took a week for the *ANW* casting group to contact the 90 to 100 applicants who would get a shot to run on the qualifier course. I had been added to a private Facebook group whose members were ninja hopefuls who had completed applications and sent in submission videos for consideration for the

2016 season. We all eagerly awaited that 818 area code call that could indicate we had been invited. During that period I was glued to my phone and that Facebook application. My emotions during that time were tremendously strong: hopes and doubts, and doubts and hopes, back and forth.

The Sting!

I will share more of that experience later in the book, but I'm going to skip to the end result: After a few weeks I finally received confirmation (through some of Michelle's producer contacts) that I would *not* be invited to compete that year.

The no was hard to swallow. It stings to hear no about anything. It hurt being rejected after all the mental and physical preparation and effort I had put in for over a year and a half. Like any sting, it hurt the most right after the initial news and shock. The pain lessened over time, eased by the fact that the calls were coming more slowly and to fewer people near the end of the process. The "no" answer sent me into an evaluation of what the past 18 months of training had been worth. The longer I focused on that question the more I gained perspective and an appreciation of my real goals.

I Won

Yes, I wanted the opportunity to compete on an *ANW* course, but I really had much bigger goals that I definitely achieved. In the midst of the disappointment it began to hit me clearly — I had won, and I won big! If I focused on what I was able to control, which was not whether I was selected by NBC for the show, I had a fantastic 18 months, and I won.

The Letter

To stay focused, and to share the news with those who encouraged and supported me during that time, hoping so much for me to get a chance to run, I posted a response on Facebook. It basically said, "No, I wasn't invited to run, I'm okay, and I really won." Below is the Facebook message I shared with my family, friends, and supporters:

2016 *American Ninja Warrior* Update

I understand it is now official. My four month wait since I submitted my application and video to *ANW* has now come to a close. The invitation calls have ended and I wasn't one of the few who were selected to compete this year on *ANW*.

I'm now experiencing some disappointment, frustration, and relief. My mind is finally at ease knowing my destiny relative to the course. I no longer need to process in my mind how I will do and my strategy for each of the obstacles, starting with the new version of the steps that was used on the course.

I am one of the over 75,000 people who have trained and took the time to submit an *ANW* application and video. About 500 people were selected to compete, across five cities. There were so many who had worked hard to improve their skills who will not run in 2016, just like the prior seven years. I hope all of us in this category are as pleased as I am for the growth that I've seen in my life during my past two years of training.

These two years have been fun and intensive. I do not regret anything that I've done. I have won, relative to the commitment that I made to myself and my daughter two years ago. I successfully completed my commitment to train that 57-year-old body hard for two years, produce a submission video displaying my skill and story, and submit it to *ANW* by the due date to compete, in 2016, when I'm age 59. Completed! Successful! I'm proud that I was able to stay focused and accomplish that.

Over these past two years I've invested well over 1,000 hours of physical training, several hundreds of dollars on equipment (in the house, basement, garage, yard, and car), and I've learned so much strategy and technique about how to approach obstacles. I've sacrificed a number of other commitments, events, and experiences in order to prioritize my ninja training.

I'm much healthier than I was two years ago. This includes significantly increasing my strength in my arms, fingers, and legs. I've won. I have much greater flexibility and stretching capability. I have significantly better balance. I have greater agility with my feet. I've won. I have a much stronger body core. I also have significant calluses on my hands.☺ I've modified my diet and also lost over 10 pounds. I have won. I've learned how to use the iMovie application to produce a video. That was a fun learning process. (This application has more features and ease-of-use than the editors I used 30 years ago when I graduated with a radio and TV broadcasting degree from college.) I've met so many new friends through that effort. I value these relationships and will continue to nurture many of them for years to come. I've won.

To face facts, I have had multiple injuries, in six different places, including my hamstring muscles, groin, calf, back, right shoulder, and lower abdomen. It had been a challenging year on that front. I've also just learned to live sore and aching. It's going to feel good to just feel normal again as I back down my training going forward. I will still train, and have fun, but at a much more relaxed and fun pace, producing, I hope, many fewer injuries.

I've learned that my great story (59-year-old, retiree, dad of Michelle Warnky, mini-stroke, professional coach, with no previous sports background) wasn't as good of a story as those that we will have the opportunity to hear and enjoy on the show. There are so many fantastic people out there. As much as I would have loved to compete on the course, I'm sure that NBC made good choices to be able to share some great stories and performances in season eight.

What do I now gain with this news? I get some time back. I hope my soreness and aches will reduce. I anticipate some better sleep, based on less soreness. There will be less money spent on equipment and I'll take a little less ibuprofen for those times of pain and recovery.

I will keep many of the habits and routines that I've developed over these recent years, including much of my diet, core exercises, stretching, and fun times at the gym, setting new personal records on many of the obstacles: one more peg on the rings obstacle, four more inches on the cliffhanger, two more feet on the slack line, etc. Each of these have made me better and are creating a better future for me.

Thanks so much to my wife, Carolyn, for all of her support during this window of time. It has taken a tremendous amount of my focus. Thanks also to Michelle and many other ninjas who have contributed to my growth.

I've learned so much and I had a lot of fun through this experience. I hope and pray you continue to invest in yourself and enjoy the process of personal growth.

I felt good about my message. It revealed my perspective and my heart. I won! I won especially in relation to my goals that were truly under my control. You could say I had even hit a home run.

13 Reasons

At the beginning of my training I documented 13 reasons I was going to train, and reviewed it at least once a month during the 18-month period. I found that clearly defining and documenting my "reasons" has been very helpful in keeping me focused and on track whenever I want to accomplish something.

My "Reasons to Ninja Train" List:

- Ramp up the focus on my health
- Follow through on my initial commitment and announcement to others
- Be an encourager and challenger of others
- Be an inspiration to others
- Have fun running on obstacles (Arches National Park on steroids)
- Be the oldest man up the warped wall
- Create more family events
- Have fun spending more time with Michelle
- Push my limits, physically and mentally
- Gain exposure for my Well Done Life business
- Create the possibility to be on TV; notoriety; recognition
- Experience the novelty
- Win a million dollars

These reasons kept me focused and going during the ups and downs of my 18 months of training. There were plenty of ups and downs in respect to my other life commitments, priorities, and injuries that occurred during that time.

What are the reasons for your goals?

In the following four chapters I share insights on how I won with my ninja training. I also dive deeper into each of my 13 reasons to train, and I share more about how they helped me stay focused and motivated. How did they help me? Read on!

13 Reasons to Train

My Reasons 1–4

1. To Ramp Up the Focus on My Health

My health is the best that it has ever been. I've significantly improved my leg, arm, and finger strength. My core is radically stronger. I've improved my balance tremendously. My agility and reaction time are much better. I now know how to safely and confidently fall from an obstacle so I don't hurt myself, and I've greatly reduced my risk of falling while doing everyday activities. I'm in much better condition than I was when I started ninja training. I absolutely won in this category!

How is your health? I encourage you to take great care of your body and give it the attention it needs. When your health is poor every part of your body pays the price. When you're weak or sick the point is very clear that your body must be your first priority!

How healthy are you? Are you taking good care of yourself? I sure hope so. This is the body or house that you will live in for the rest of your life. Take very good care of it so that you can enjoy it for the rest of your life.

2. To Follow Through on My Initial Commitment and Announcement to Others

My word, what I commit to do in front of others, is very important to me. I made a commitment to Michelle to train the best I could to be prepared to create a quality submission video for *ANW*. I committed to representing myself and our family well at age 58. I took that commitment seriously, stayed focused, and followed through. I reaped so many benefits because of it. This is an absolute A on the grading scale. It's a big win in following through on my word to myself and others, which impacts so much of the rest of my life. When we know that we will do what we say we will do, it positively spills into all other aspects of our lives.

I follow through on my commitments and remain focused on living each day in such a way that my Creator/God is able to say to me each evening, "Well done, Good and Faithful Servant." This is my heart's desire, from the Bible passage Matthew 25:21. In my heart I've heard that message from my Creator/God. I'm so thankful.

How well do you follow through on what you say you will do? Your ability to do what you say you will do impacts your confidence in yourself and your entire outlook on life. It impacts your confidence in who you are and in what you can do. When you can't trust yourself, you don't trust others either. The ability to consistently follow through on what we say we will do is a very powerful trait.

3. To Be an Encourager and Challenger of Others

I've encouraged and challenged others through my exposure on the show, by participating and cheering at competitions, by training side by side with other ninjas, and even through my posts on Facebook, Instagram, and LinkedIn. I have revealed my heart and life to others, helping encourage and challenge them to move forward with their lives and goals.

I'm an imperfect guy. At times I seem to continue to make wrong, selfish choices. I'm still able to live my imperfect life in peace since I have confidence in the forgiveness that I've received from God through the sacrificial death of Jesus, who died on the cross to pay my penalty for all the times I've lived below our Holy God's perfect standard. I'm so thankful for His forgiveness and the peace He has provided. I want that same experience and relationship with Him for everyone.

I feel so good when I get to encourage and challenge others to live better lives. My hope is that others have a living and active relationship with our Creator/God and with all people. I believe that God has significantly grown and developed me and I feel responsible for revealing that growth and modeling it for others in how I live my life.

My Deepest Heart Topics

Here are a few of the most important topics in my heart:

- Having a relationship with our amazing and loving Creator
- Having great and strong loving family relationships

- Listening well to others
- Reflecting, planning, and making good choices
- Encouraging others during their life challenges
- Having the power to move through life challenges that we experience, like the mini-stroke that I had in 2012
- Being active and exercising to stay strong physically
- Learning, trying, and accomplishing new things that I had never dreamed I could do

How could you have a positive impact on others? Tell others the things that are in your heart, the things that you feel matter. You can make a significant difference in the lives of others.

4. To Be an Inspiration to Others

It's so encouraging and motivating when I see someone doing something I have never done and that I want to do. This is definitely the case with ninja warrior. Seeing people like Kelvin Antoine (Grandpa Ninja), Michael Moore, Jon Stewart, and many others compete on *ANW*, I've been encouraged that maybe I could too.

We each know people we impact. I influence people that my ninja friends don't know, and they influence people I don't know. I want to be an inspiration to the people in my world. To do that I share both my successes and failures through various Facebook, Instagram, and LinkedIn posts. The response from family, friends, and others has been tremendous. They have shared how they have been encouraged and motivated to continue or to try things they haven't done before.

Who could you be an inspiration to if you were to ninja train? Would you like knowing that people see you as a ninja, someone who is growing, having more fun, and getting healthier?

You Matter

We all want to matter – to do something that has an influence beyond ourselves. This may just be the opportunity for you to get out there and have fun on a ninja obstacle and inspire someone. It could be your family or friends. You could even positively impact people you don't even know, people who see you from a distance. You can make a difference. It could bring smiles to their faces and could even make them say, "Can I do that? That looks so fun!"

Chapter 4

My Reasons 5–8

5. To Have Fun Running on Obstacles

Do you like to travel and see exciting new places on this earth? It is an amazing world that we live in. Carolyn and I have traveled across the U.S. and to Europe, Central America, South America, and Asia. We have been to some amazing places. Of all of these places, I enjoy Arches National Park in Moab, Utah, the most. If you have not been there, you have to check it out. To me it is awe-inspiring, beautiful, and just plain fun!

It's my favorite place on the planet. I love the red-colored rock, the blue sky, and yes, generally even the heat. (My wife has a different view about the over-
100-degree temperatures that we often experienced when we were there in the summer.)

Arches is special because there are so many places to hike, climb, descend, jump across, and squeeze through. It's so much fun to explore that portion of our earth. My favorite spot is at the back of the park, 18 miles in, where you can hike to the Double O Arches. It's such a fun hike with so much to explore and do along the way.

Ninja Gyms

I live in Columbus, Ohio, not at Arches National Park, which is more than 20 driving hours away in Moab, Utah. In Ohio I might not get the big desert sky and the heat, but I do get to enjoy the colors in the various ninja gyms. They're all different. And I love to climb, descend, swing, jump, and roll at each of these gyms. It's so much fun, pushing myself to see if I can balance a little longer or farther on a unique obstacle, swing across a wider span, jump to a new height, or drop to a new distance on the floor, all safely without getting hurt.

These gyms provide a taste of Arches National Park at home. They even give me more options for things to play and try than the fabulous Arches environment. And they are a lot safer than some of the things I try at Arches, which is a good thing at my age. Training as a ninja has been a blast, which is a good reason for continuing with this level of exercise.

When and where do you get fun and movement? If you don't regularly move, I encourage you to be sure to add it to your life. There are so many options. Here are a few: You can swim, play ping pong, play volleyball, shoot some basketball baskets, or even visit a local ninja gym and play like I do. Movement is so important to our health. Find a way to play and move at the same time.

6. To Be the Oldest Man Up the Warped Wall

It's always fun to reach new milestones and do something that I've never done. What if we could accomplish something no one has ever done? That would be very cool!

When I first wrote this book, I had the potential to be the first 60-year-old to make it to the top of an *ANW* warped wall. Now that's something worth training for! It's good to have a dream or a big goal to help keep you focused. This one worked well for me.

At that time, the oldest person to catch the top of the warped wall was 54-year-old Jon Stewart. Jon is an amazing ninja, and an encouraging friend. I'm confident that he will be able to make it to the top of the warped wall when he turns 60, but that is in the future. I'm sure many other current ninjas will be able to do it when they turn 60; people like Drew Drechsel, in 25 to 30 years from now.

To be the first to stick the top of the wall at my age, I needed to be invited to compete or wait in the walk-on line in hopes of getting an opportunity to run. That did not happen in 2016. In 2017 I did join the walk-on line and I did get to compete. You can read about my 2017 *ANW* Cleveland walk-on line experience in *What Just Happened?: The Line*. And you can learn about my course-run experience in *What Just Happened?: The Run*.

At times I've been able to repeatedly stick the top of two 14-foot warped walls in local gyms. And these walls have been steeper than those currently used on the show – anything is possible! I also realize that now the wall on the show is 14-and-a-half feet high.

What unique opportunities do you have? What would be a stretch for you? Goals that stretch us can be very energizing and motivating.

I encourage you to find a fun and enjoyable stretch goal that would be special, just for you.

7. To Create More Family Events

What are your favorite family events? Carolyn and I have turned *ANW* competitions and local ninja warrior competitions into family events, often traveling to cheer on Michelle as she competes across

the U.S. She has also competed internationally in China and in Malaysia, though we didn't make those trips.

Over the years many family members have been with us as Michelle competed in competitions including ninja warrior, Spartan races, and many other Obstacle Course Races (OCR). My parents, Russ and Carolyn; our son, Tim, and his wife, Bonnie; and aunts and uncles and even cousins have joined us for this ninja-style family fun!

My competing on an *ANW* qualifying course would take our family participation to a whole new level, drawing even more family members. And it did in Cleveland in 2017. It's so good to have family – and many friends who now feel like family – rally around my efforts.

Who would rally around you if you started to train as a ninja? You might be surprised by how many family and friends would take a strong interest and be there to cheer you on as you train and compete in local competitions and maybe even on *ANW*. You would be amazed at the welcoming and supportive nature of the ninja community. New friends abound!

8. To Have Fun Spending More Time with Michelle

How do you spend time with your family? Training as a ninja means that I'm investing even more in Michelle. She is very engaged in ninja warrior through her gym and the many competitions she competes in or conducts. It's tremendous when a parent engages in activities that are important to their kids. It's even better when it's fun and healthy for the parent.

Michelle frequently travels to compete in competitions. She speaks across the country, and she successfully manages her ninja gym. Although it's tough to catch her these days, my engagement in ninja warrior has allowed me to spend more time with her than I would have. I'm grateful for that time! Becoming a competitor has opened the door for us to interact with a new and different perspective.

I thought I would be able to spend more time with her playing and training on obstacles. As most ninja gym owners know, owning a gym does not mean you will be able to sustain or increase your personal training time, even though you have obstacles at your disposal. Owning a gym usually reduces your training time because your focus has to be on gym-related responsibilities and priorities. These include class structure; staffing, designing, and setting up competitions; various marketing activities; building new obstacles; figuring out ways to better use your available gym space; evaluating

future expansion; conducting personal client training; managing payroll and administrative tasks; and much more.

How can training as a ninja increase your interaction time with a family member or friend? How could that time you spend together be better if you were having more fun and feeling happier and better about yourself?

.

Chapter 5

Reasons 9 and 10

9. To Push My Limits, Physically and Mentally

What new things have you recently accomplished? I love pushing my limits. When Tim and Michelle were in grade school, and then also in high school at Thomas Worthington in Worthington, Ohio, our focus was always on setting a "PR," a personal record, especially in cross-country or track events. A PR is going where you've never gone before, exploring new territory or new ground.

In cross-country, your PR was your fastest time for completing a course. We loved to celebrate not only with our kids, but also with other members of the cross-country team. It was just as big a deal when Lauren Birnie, Jenny Brill, or Rebecca Price set a new PR. Even when our kids were in grade school we celebrated PRs.

Frosty! Frosty! Frosty!

I remember one of Michelle's races in middle school. She knew if she set a PR she would earn a small Wendy's Frosty as her reward. The rest of the team also knew about her reward system. Near the end of the race, team members joined us in cheering, "Frosty, Frosty, Frosty!" And of course she poured it on at the end and earned another PR, and – yes – another Frosty. She earned many Frostys over those years.

At some point the Wendy's Frosty grew to a Dairy Queen Blizzard®. I don't remember what year we made that transition. It was worth it to see Tim and Michelle and their teammates strive to set PRs. The reward wasn't

for coming in first, second, or third place, or scoring a number of points for the team. It was based on improving one's own personal performance, getting a little bit better or faster. This is the best competition – the one with yourself. It's doing what you can to improve something that you control – yourself and your performance – based on how hard and consistently you work at it.

Ninja PRs

Ninja training has allowed me to set new PRs. At a ninja gym the PR potential is unlimited. I can set PRs for so many types of runs, jumps, swings, climbs, descends, and much more. I don't buy myself a DQ Blizzard every time I set a PR, but I have done that a few times to celebrate a new personal achievement level.

I'm aware of personal best performances in all my playing and training. I celebrate both small and big improvements on any obstacle or training skill. When I first started training I wasn't able to catch and hold the top of the 14-foot warped wall. It took me over 1,000 attempts to finally catch the top of the wall for the first time. At one point I stuck it three times in the same open gym! At another point my ratio of catching the top of the warped wall was closer to 50 percent. This was a major improvement and accomplishment. That is progress, and worth celebrating! As you can imagine, my health has a big impact on my ability to stick the top of the wall. If I'm injured in some way it is much more difficult to catch that top.

How high is 14 feet? When Carolyn and I were driving in Michigan, some of the bridges we drove under stated the maximum height for a

vehicle to drive under the bridge. The clearance for the bridge in this picture is 14 feet. When I noticed that sign it hit me just how high a warped wall really is. It's a big challenge to run up a steep wall, reach the top (at 14 feet or higher), and hold on.

Mental Challenge

Going for PRs is not just a physical activity. It is probably even more of a mental exercise. I really enjoy that quote from Yogi Berra: "Baseball is ninety percent mental. The other half is physical." I think that applies to ninja skills and competitions as well.

So much of the progress on ninja obstacles comes down to: Are you willing in your mind to commit to doing something with all you have, without hesitation? Do you see yourself being able to meet the challenge in your mind? As Henry Ford once said, "If you think you can, or if you think you can't, you're right." I've found that to be true on many ninja obstacles.

What You Can and Can't Do

So often we limit ourselves by thinking we can't do something, even when we can. We don't even try, thinking it's impossible instead of chipping away at it, moving toward eventual success. I've observed many new ninjas who I believe *can* probably do something, but they don't *think* they can. The biggest battle is with our mind, not our physical skill. My training has helped challenge and sharpen my mind regarding what I can and can't do... YET.

Writing this book is an excellent example. A few years ago I never would have guessed that I would be writing a book, and now I've written and published four books. Once that seemed like an impossibility. Now it is a reality and I have plans to write at least another 11 books.

Self-Talk

Think of a situation in which you faced a challenge. Did you have negative self-talk that shut you down? Did you hear your mind saying, "I can't," or "I could never do that"? These critical and judgmental thoughts will get in your way, if you allow them. They will tell you that you're not good enough. If you take these words to heart and act on them, you will never reach your potential.

Do you trust your inner voice when it's hurting you? At that time are you listening to the voice of a friend or an enemy? A friend will stand by your side, believe in you, and be there to support you in any way they can. An enemy is critical, judging, and makes mean com-

ments about your every move or thought. Even though your critical inner voice can feel true, step back and stop listening to that voice if it's holding you back. Listen to the best friend in your mind, not the enemy who wants to prevent you from moving forward.

With the support of a friend or family member by our side, believing in us, most of us have experienced some success with something new or challenging that we have taken on. Positive support like that is so powerful! You can provide that same support to yourself through what you allow your mind to say to you. Spend your time with your best friend, not the enemy who wants you to fail. You wouldn't intentionally spend time with an enemy who is critical of you, so don't let that happen on your inside, in your thinking.

Facing ninja obstacles with supportive friends – and the friend perspective in my mind – has helped me see that I have more potential than I could possibly have imagined.

You Can Do It!

By focusing on your potential, seeing yourself be successful, and ensuring you believe in yourself, you can create and meet new personal milestones. When those doubts come in, say to yourself, "I can do this! I got this!" You can do it! Go out there and set some new PRs in your life. When you do, you experience the excitement of traveling to a new and exciting place, and that opens more doors of possibility and opportunity for you.

10. To Gain Exposure for my Well Done Life Business

How many people do you think watch *ANW*? It's over six million people. That kind of exposure could be helpful for my executive- and life-coaching business. This is not one of my primary motives, but it is one more reason to train as a ninja and for the show.

NBC Exposure – The Encouraging Dad

I've had a good deal of exposure on NBC. I've been highlighted many times on *ANW* as "the encourager dad" of ninja Michelle Warnky. Carolyn and I've been front and center for multiple years at ninja competitions. People have recognized me from the show as I've traveled across the country.

At a local chamber of commerce meeting, a woman looked at me and said, "I think I know you from somewhere." We talked about the places I had worked and churches I had attended. She said, "No. It's from somewhere else." I thought to myself, *Should I go down the* ANW *path with her?* I decided I would. I asked, "Do you watch TV?" She answered, "Yes." Then I asked, "Have you seen *American Nin...*?" She jumped all over my question with an exuberant reply: "You're him! You're the dad of the girl from Columbus on the show! I'm so excited! Can I give you a hug? I love that show!" This is just one more example of how exposure on the show can boost your familiarity, relationship to, and respect from others.

Well Done Life® LLC

I'm a professional life coach. My business is called Well Done Life. I help people when they're feeling stuck with an important issue in their lives or business-es. I work one on one with indi-viduals. I'm also a motivational speaker. I work part time so I can spend a good deal of my time writ-ing books, ninja training, traveling, enjoying time with family, and volunteering. I truly want to be a very happy retired, or "pro-tired" guy, as I describe it.

Exposure for my business on *ANW* could increase my opportuni-ties to help many more people. How could you impact others more significantly?

Chapter 6

Reasons 11–13

11. To Create the Possibility to Be on TV; Notoriety; Recognition

Have you been recognized by others for your ability to run fast, climb, sing, play an instrument, draw or paint, write, or because you know a lot about a particular topic?

Carolyn and I were at a restaurant in Lakeland, Florida, having lunch, when a waitress asked, "Aren't you the dad on *American Ninja Warrior*? I love that show. It's fun to see you cheering on your daughter and others."

Being on TV and being recognized is a great conversation starter. For those who would rather not be recognized, including Carolyn, this type of exposure can be overwhelming. The power of exposure on a major network TV show is unbelievable when it comes to the respect and relationship it can create with people from across the country.

In Los Angeles, at the *Team Ninja Warrior* season one site, Eric Gates, a new ninja at the time, came up to me while we were waiting in line to get onto the set and asked, "Can I get a picture with you? You're my favorite *American Ninja Warrior* fan on the side-lines." I like the reputation of being supportive and encouraging.

Getting to run the course, and being featured on NBC, would provide more of these fun experiences and give me the opportunity to encourage even more people. I would also be able to share my experience and story in more detail if I got the chance to bring attention to my *Heart of a Ninja Series* ninja books.

This one is also not a big motivator for my training, but it would be a blast for me and my family. I don't want my personal sense of value to come from the recognition of others. I believe I was personally designed and created by my loving God and that gives me my sense of value. I'm confident He wants a relationship with me and that He loves to see when I use the abilities and skills He has given and developed in me to positively impact others, which I believe brings Him glory. I want to live my life in a way that He can say to me, "Well done, Good and Faithful Servant."

Where do you get your sense of value? I hope you also get it through our loving Creator/God.

12. To Experience the Novelty

Dictionary.com defines *novelty* as:

1. The quality of being new, original, or unusual.
   Synonyms: originality, newness, freshness, unconventionality, unfamiliarity
2. a small and inexpensive toy or ornament.

I wasn't thinking in terms of being "a small and inexpensive toy or ornament," but rather "new, original, or unusual." I can be original and unusual in that I retired at age 56, I have a daughter who competes on *ANW*, and I'm convinced I can beat the warped wall on an *ANW* course. That would be pretty novel. Many of the other reasons to train are much more important to me.

What are you doing that is novel, new, original, or unusual? Doing something new brings new life as you stretch and experience something for the first time. It's invigorating! I encourage you to enjoy the stimulation of trying something new. Who knows, maybe I will run into you at a ninja gym one of these days.

13. To Win a Million Dollars

I did not win a million dollars. I wasn't that disappointed in that miss; so much of it was not in my control. But I did have to put this on the list, right? That is why some others train.

I gained a whole lot more than a million dollars of value from my training when I consider the accomplishments I've listed, especially with my health and the relationships I've been able to build.

I love what John Maxwell said: "Many people will spend all of their health to get wealth, and once they have wealth, they would give all of that wealth to get back their health." I would love to have both, but I put health above wealth. And from my perspective, I'm a very wealthy individual, in big part because of my good health.

You can tell that I love quotes, and I love this one: "The richest man is not he who has the most, but he who needs the least." I hope I'm being more content in all situations. Being content has been very powerful, and that includes not being invited to compete on *ANW*.

Ups and Downs

I've had a lot of powerful reasons to support me through my training – and there have been a lot of ups and downs. There have been times when I set three or four new PRs in one day, going farther in a competition, or farther than I had ever dreamed. There have also been times when the obstacles just seemed too hard to beat – too far for my reach, too difficult to hang on holding my whole body –

just plain too hard, causing me to feel, "I can't do it!" I've also had physical injuries during that time. With experience and learning, I've had fewer injuries than I did when I started. I'm learning and growing.

"Yet"

With these powerful reasons, my "I can't do it!" has become "I can't do it... yet." And that is a tremendous difference. That is *all* the difference. One position reflects no hope, and the other says there is hope and I will get there – I just need more time and work.

Who would have dreamed that the little word *yet* could be so powerful? It is an extremely powerful, tiny word that packs a big punch. To be able to think and then verbally say the word *yet* injects hope and a desired future into our lives.

I'm not suggesting that the word *yet* applies to everything, but I believe it can apply to a whole lot more things than many of us think. Ninja training has helped me see the "yet" concept come to life for me and many of my peers. Two examples are my experience on the warped wall and swinging between elevated bars. When I first started training, I was three feet short of the top on my warped wall attempts, and I could only *lache*, or swing across one bar to another bar, with short distances between the bars. My warped wall catches are now much more consistent, and sometimes I can complete laches with eight-foot gaps between the bars. And I'm not even six feet tall. Eight feet is a very long way to fly through the air when you're swinging on those bars.

"Yet" Has Served Me Well

I still have a lot of *yets* in my life, as a ninja and in many other respects. On the ninja front, I cannot yet catch the top of a warped wall every time, but I'm getting closer to that level. I'm not yet as consistent as I want to be on an eight-foot lache. I'm not yet able to move up (and especially come down) a salmon ladder with the consistency I would like. I'm not yet consistent in walking across a 10-foot slack line. But I'm much, much, closer than I was in the past. My key word is *yet*. It has served me well in the past and I know it will serve me very well in the future.

The same could be said about writing a book. When I finished the first draft of *The Heart of a Ninja*, I had not yet successfully written a book. As you can see, now I have published that book and three other books, and you're reading the product of one of my prior "yets."

Where do you need to start adding the word *yet*? See how it can help your mind and your actions. I'm confident that *yet* will help you.

Your Reasons

After reading my 13 reasons, what reasons can you come up with to help you achieve a goal or overcome an obstacle? The bigger your reasons the more powerful they are when you face challenges. They help you push through. The more reasons I have, the more strength I have to stay with it, keep going, and get to my goal.

Where in your life today are you saying to yourself, "I can't," and you need to add the word *yet*?

Having become a ninja and having had so many experiences with other ninjas, I have seen what I now call the heart of a ninja. In the next section I share some insights about having the heart of a ninja.

12 Traits of a Ninja

What is in the heart of a ninja? What do we feel? How do we think? Do we all feel and think the same, or differently? If we have some common traits, what are they?

Ninja Traits

Based on my experience and my exposure to hundreds of ninjas, I believe there are a number of traits that most ninjas share. I have identified 12 core traits of a ninjas. I live or try to live each of these traits myself.

I grouped these traits into three major categories: "Obstacles," "The Right Environment," and "Study" – each has four traits. I hope this list is helpful. I hope you decide to grow in these traits as well.

Chapter 7

Obstacles –
Traits 1 and 2

1. The Desire to Take on Obstacles

A Negative Image

What do you think if you hear someone talking about dealing with an obstacle in their life? The word *obstacle* can have a negative image. It's something that gets in the way, a problem we have to face. Obstacles to living the way we want to live – "life obstacles" – are less visible than ninja obstacles. They can be complex, which can make them difficult to solve. A life obstacle prevents us from moving forward. We must take on that obstacle and beat it to be able to move on. We can learn a lot from the ninja mindset, using ninja obstacles as examples of how we approach our life obstacles.

I seem to want to avoid life obstacles and not deal with them. As an example, I don't like to update my business finances on a monthly basis. I don't do it often so I'm not very efficient when I do it. For my business I just want to have the fun of coaching people to have a better life. I see the administrative part of my business as an obstacle that I have to do.

I need to better see my obstacles as things that must be addressed to move forward. Having the mind of a ninja can be helpful in identifying better ways to overcome them. I need to more consistently find ways to deal with them by playing with them and making them more fun.

Hunger

I enjoy watching ninjas approach obstacles. They hunger to face and take on an obstacle to see if they can beat it. They have a hunger to study how they and other ninjas have beaten it; a hunger for more information, or "beta" insights from people who test the obstacles; and they have a hunger to exchange ideas and approaches to find the best way to beat the obstacle.

It's fun to watch ninjas intensely observe testers as they go through an *ANW* course. I've been in Las Vegas when ninjas (I won't mention any names) just happened to be walking by the course, which is surrounded by a chain-link fence and blocked by dark tarps to prevent outsiders from seeing the course. Some of them will get down on their hands and knees, or down on the ground like an alligator, to move along the fence below the black tarps, doing all they can to see how a tester is performing on the course. This doesn't usually last long before a security guard sees them and tells them to move along. (They might not look like ninjas, but I can identify them!) They want to observe all they can of someone else's attempts to beat the obstacles. They're hungry to learn more that could be helpful when they get their chance to run the course. Many ninjas who either were not invited to compete that year or did not qualify for the finals will pay their own traveling expenses for a chance to test an obstacle at the Las Vegas *ANW* venue.

How do you approach your life obstacles? Do you do it with the mind of a ninja? Do you know you can find a way to beat them? Do you hunger to prove yourself by taking on that obstacle?

My 54-Day Cold

My latest obstacle was a 54-day cold that just kept hanging on. I approached it like a ninja, but I also just wanted to be over it. The ninja mindset opens you to a whole new approach and expectation. Rather than  dreading the cold, I needed to consider other options for addressing it. In addition to rest and liquids, I needed to be open to suggestions from friends and family rather than disregarding them, thinking they wouldn't help. Do you sometimes have a closed mind about what will and will not help you?

I also needed to acknowledge the good that could come from that time. I needed to appreciate the benefits of rest and downtime for my body. I can be so activity-based, acting as though I value *doing* things over the amazing miracle of being alive. Life is valuable in itself, but I have had a tendency to see growth and activity as more valuable. The ninja experience has helped me see that *life just for life's sake* is important. I need to remember that God has allowed me to experience illness, and I need to value that for the important lessons I can learn from it.

Can you apply the heart of a ninja to an obstacle you're facing? How could it be helpful and stimulating for you? It's a much better approach than feeling dread and being overwhelmed. It can be so powerful to say to yourself, "I can take on this obstacle and beat it, whatever it may be."

2. The Desire to Stretch and See How Much You Can Grow

How often do you stretch? (I don't mean physically, though physical stretching can also help.) How often do you try something new or try something in a different way than you have done it in the past? What are you doing to stretch and grow yourself? When was the last time you set a PR (personal record)?

Your PRs

A PR can be how fast you can finish your homework, how fast you can make a sandwich, how fast you can do five push-ups, or how many you can do. Gaining efficiency and strength can be very reward-ing. I get excited every time I set and achieve a new PR because I've improved myself with a new skill or ability.

What PRs have you recently set? What PRs could you and would you like to set? What PRs would be most helpful to you? Consider creating some new goals and working to set new PRs. They're powerful tools for helping you stretch and grow. Each time you do, it provides a tremendous feeling of excite-ment.

Ninjas always look for new ways to take on an obstacle. They say, "I wonder if I could beat that obstacle if I changed my approach?" This perspective can apply to well over 100 obstacles in most ninja gyms: "I wonder if I could skip the second cannon ball and go for the third one. Would it help me get through the obstacle better or faster?" (A cannon ball is a large hanging ball; the challenge is in grabbing a sphere rather than some-thing easier like a rope or a bar.) "I wonder if I could run down just the left side of the slanted steps," which is now done regularly by some of the top ninjas." Being open and flexible about new approaches is standard for a ninja.

Exploring Options

It's inspiring to hear a ninja say, "What if I two-step the warped wall rather than using three or four steps like most ninjas?" Or, "What if I quickly *match* (grab with both hands) on the rings rather than swing across with one hand on each ring?" The ideas that come to mind and are often attempted are so fun to see and try myself. The creativity is amazing!

Another example is on the quintuple steps – a version of the steps that have been the first obstacle on the show for years and which you can see in ninja gyms around the country. These steps are set so

that you jump back and forth, left and right, across multiple steps. During a practice time ninja Dennis Lappin and others at the Classic City Center ninja course in Waterloo, Indiana, used their agility and speed to skip the second step altogether and instead ran from the first to the third step, continuing along to the fourth and fifth steps to finally jump to the landing pad. By doing that they were able to trim their run times by a second or two by not jumping back and forth twice. It also provided them with more momentum to quickly leap to the landing pad.

It's a lot of fun to listen to the ninjas talking about it and then see them experiment with their ideas to see if they can be successful. Planning ahead for the most efficient approach is key for success. Sometimes our plans work... and sometimes they don't. Figuring out whether or not the new approach or technique provides an advantage is always on the mind of a ninja.

I Couldn't... Yet

I tried the skipping-the-second-step method, like Dennis and others had been doing, and I couldn't do it. To be successful, I had to jump to my right and land with my left foot on the first step rather than the more natural outside or right foot. That was way too uncomfortable at that point in my development. I couldn't do it – yet – in the short time I had to prepare for the competition the next day. It's best to do what  you find works best for you. A technique that works well for one ninja with their body type might not be the best approach for another. I've learned to listen to my body as I try to find approaches that work best. It's a process to learn and grow in these ways.

Working Up to It

In the past I have not been a very flexible guy. My legs are quite tight, so I do not yet have the stride and leg power of many of my fellow younger ninjas. This is a good example of getting to know my body, listening to it, and not pushing too hard too quickly, which can result in an injury. This doesn't mean that I don't push myself. It means that I'm cautious and careful when trying new things and that I may take a different approach based on what I've learned about my body at my age. I want to develop the ability to do many of these moves, but I must work up to them.

Do you want to stretch? The first step is to set some goals and strive to reach some new PRs. I encourage you to stretch and see what you can do that you have never done before.

Obstacles – Traits 3 and 4

3. It's You versus the Obstacle, Not Others

Comparing Yourself to Others

When do you compare yourself to others? How does that comparison help you or hurt you? For many of us it can cause negative feelings. We compare the greatest strength of others to our average strength or weakness. When we do that, it's easy to get discouraged.

I love the fact that most ninjas approach the sport with a "me versus the obstacle" mindset rather than "me versus someone else." You only control yourself, not others. If you want to improve what you control, focus on yourself and not on others. You can learn and grow from the experience of others without comparing your performance with theirs. This ninja trait has helped me avoid comparing myself to others.

Focus on What You Control

When you focus on yourself and the obstacle instead of someone else, you have much better control of the results. You can study the obstacle and evaluate your abilities relative to it. On a ninja course that can be focusing on your balance skills, including your ability on rolling objects, wobbly objects, bouncy objects, and sinking or soft objects. These are just a few examples. When your focus is on the requirements of the

obstacle and your skill level, you're truly productive. Your mind can evaluate your best options and how to best use the options.

Prioritize

All of my ninja skills need improvement. When I train I prioritize balance, core strength, and finger strength. I usually spend time on at least two balance obstacles. In addition, I often do what I call "knee-ups" to strengthen my core; as I perform a pull-up I also pull my knees up to the bar. I also do dead hangs on various obstacles, hanging by one or two hands from a bar, a rock-climbing hold, a ring, a

peg, a cannon ball, or whatever. Building my skills in many areas puts me in a better position to beat many types of obstacles and it allows me to have more fun and play longer on a course run.

Focusing on the obstacles and your current skill level is a more productive way to live life and also to compete in a ninja competition. It's so much more beneficial for you than comparing yourself to others.

What skills are you developing? How much better prepared could you be to face life and ninja obstacles if you worked harder at developing additional skills?

4. The Knowledge that Every Obstacle Is Different

Are all obstacles in life and on ninja courses the same? Absolutely not! With ninja warrior you will face both different obstacles and obstacles that are similar yet different in some way. There are some standard obstacles that appear on every *ANW* city qualifier course. The first obstacle is always some type of steps and the warped wall is the last obstacle. Over the years, even these obstacles have changed slightly, which has been enough to make them a lot harder for some ninjas. On city finals courses, the salmon ladder has always come after the warped wall.

Most of the other obstacles are different from course to course. Some are brand new and some are similar to obstacles used on other courses or in past years but with some new twist: a little farther apart, higher, having a greater tilt, a narrower or wider hold, a rope instead of a pole, rising instead of flat – you name it. Something is going to be different, which adds to the excitement.

City Qualifier to Finals

Changes are made to the course between the city qualifier round and the finals round. There might be the same obstacles, in the same order, but effectively the finals is a different course because some adjustments will have been made to at least a few of the obstacles. Some of the first six obstacles cannot be approached the same way the second time. In addition, there are three to four additional obstacles added to the back of the course.

This is what makes *ANW* so different from other competitions and sports. Unlike baseball, football, basketball, tennis, volleyball, and all other sports, the game changes for you every time you compete, and those quick and efficient body adjustments you have to make in a split second can make the difference in whether or not you have a successful run.

What Would It Be Like?

In baseball, what would it be like if a pitcher threw his first pitch from the normal raised pitching mound 90 feet away, then threw his second pitch from level ground and only 45 feet away, and his third pitch from the first base direction? What if during the fourth pitch there were no second base and the runner would have to run from first to third base without touching the pitcher's mound while running across the field?

What would it be like in football if on your first possession you had to go 10 yards for a first down, and on your next possession you had to go 15 yards for a first down, and the field were only half as wide?

What would it be like to never be able to step on the game ice before playing a hockey game? And to throw in a little ninja twist, this time the ice has a 5-percent uphill grade or slant from one end to the other, and the goal is half the usual size and faces sideways? And you had to use a ping pong paddle and a softball instead of a hockey stick and puck. Now that would be a good version of ninja hockey.☺

I could go on and on with examples of how other sports would look if they were conducted like *ANW*. Our sport is different and challenging in unique ways. There is no practice on the actual obstacle, you just hope your diverse training has prepared you for the exciting moment when you get to run the course and get on those cool obstacles. Once you have started a run, if you misstep or misjudge a movement or lose your grip and fall, the fun is instantly over. In our ninja world, it is "one and done." All you can do is reflect after the fact to optimize future runs. If you're on an obstacle before you're scheduled to compete, you're disqualified. Isn't that like life – surprises continually pop up all around us.

Training on Similar Obstacles

Local gyms don't normally have the funding that NBC does, but they do their best to simulate obstacles on a much smaller budget. Most of the obstacles that ninjas train on are different from those on an official *ANW* course.

Training on similar obstacles is still very helpful when it comes to developing skills and abilities, with the hope that the new skills will carry over to obstacles you might face at a local gym or on an *ANW* course. Each core skill you develop is helpful when it comes time to adapt to the peculiarities of a course. Timing, confidence, technique, strength, and speed are beneficial as new obstacles are faced. Ninjas are constantly testing and trying different types of obstacles to improve their dynamic balance; core strength; quick, light foot movements; leg power for strides and hops; arm and grip strength; and overall agility and technique.

In addition to local ninja gym classes, open gyms, and *ANW* competitions themselves, there are ninja leagues. Two of the biggest ones at this time are the National Ninja League (NNL) and the Ultimate Ninja Athlete Association (UNAA). I've participated in some of these competitions across the United States. Leagues give ninjas the opportunity to qualify at local competitions across the country for a finals competition at the end of the season, competing against the best of the best. Many of the top ninjas from *ANW* participate in at least one of the leagues.

Ninjas develop skills so they can successfully face new obstacles. Through training and preparation, many skills become natural, creating muscle memory so that the ninja can focus on the subtle

differences that happen in the moment and their body can make the necessary movements to complete an obstacle. One of the things I love about the sport is that it's a continual learning process and you never fully arrive. You can always learn to move more efficiently and gain endurance and power. The best part is that it feels so good to be strong in both my mind and body, making me the best version of myself.

Ninja Obstacles Are Like Life

Ninja obstacles are a great analogy for life obstacles. The obstacles on the course are easy to identify. Although life obstacles can be very different, they are similar in that they present a challenge we must face. In ninja competitions, the obstacles come back to back to back. It's the same in life. We don't get to practice on the exact obstacles that we face on a ninja course or in life. We must find ways to successfully get through the challenges and we must live with the results of the choices we made. Keeping ourselves healthy and having good thoughts enables us to face each of them. The lessons we learn from ninja training and competitions can help us in our daily lives.

How well do you prepare and train for obstacles in life? They can be different from what you have experienced in the past and they can come back to back to back. What skills can you develop and what training can help prepare you for overcoming life obstacles or challenges? I encourage you to develop the heart of a ninja and develop your skills so that when challenges come, you're ready to take them on and beat them.

When it comes to planting a seed, the environment is so important. Rich soil allows an acorn to grow into a mighty oak tree. In poor soil that same acorn will dry out and decay, or even be eaten by a squirrel. A healthy environment is very important for our growth and for living a healthy life. In the next chapter we'll look at living in the right environment.

Chapter 9

The Right Environment – Traits 5 and 6

5. Encouragement, Support, and Celebration

Encouragement

Where do you know you can turn in the good times and in the bad? Where do you get encouragement and support when you need it? Do you have a group that will be there for you? Some people turn to God. Some have a supportive family or group of friends. Some don't have anyone or anywhere to go to for encouragement and support... yet. How about you?

As ninjas, we are confident in our ninja community. We know the support we'll get. Ninjas like to grow, develop, push, and test themselves. We are there to support each other when we face obstacles or challenges. We thrive on exploring and expanding our boundaries, pushing past obstacles, and enjoying life to the fullest. The ninja community is so encouraging.

Support

I've been blessed to experience that level of support over and over. I've seen it at MLAB OH, Classic City Ninja Warrior, The Edge, XT Fitness, and at other ninja gyms across the country. I've seen it at *ANW* city qualifying sites and at the Las Vegas *ANW* finals site! I've even seen it at parks like the Scioto Audubon in Columbus and at Venice Beach in Los Angeles. Ninjas support and encourage each other in both their successes and failures. We relate to each other.

Celebration

I love achieving a new PR with ninjas in the gym. I remember the excitement and celebration I experienced the first time I stuck an eight-foot lache. The high fives and hoots and hollers were so fun. My ninja buddies had to remind me to celebrate the first time I made it across a difficult  narrow ledge – a longer-reach cliff-hanger obstacle. I was so focused on my technique that I didn't realize it was the first time I had cleared it. As always, celebration, high fives, and hugs followed.

And I remember the support I got at an MLAB OH ninja competition when I fell on the third obstacle, a balance tank (PVC pipe) obstacle. I felt really badly about going down early on an obstacle that I had trained for but couldn't beat that day. To lift my spirits I immediately received many hugs, high fives, and words of encouragement to keep at it and keep learning from each experience.

Vulnerability

We all can relate to experiencing both success and failure. Wouldn't it be amazing if you had this level of support from everyone you know? Ninjas put themselves out there, revealing their fears when taking on obstacles. It's scary to share our fears, but that's what it takes to be part of the ninja community. You and the obstacle are on full display for fellow ninjas and instructors. This sharing opens the door for the support we all want and need.

Where do you need to be more open and share the challenges you're facing so that you can get the support you need? Sharing fears is a key trait that the ninja environment provides. We can learn so much from sharing our concerns and fears. I encourage you to take that step to open that door for more support. The power it can provide is amazing.

6. Always Playing: Everything Is a Game

How much of your day includes play? How often do you make what you have to do a game, to see if you can do it better or faster than the last time you did it? What if that was how you approached life on a regular basis? How could that improve your life?

Dishes First

I think back to when I was in grade school, especially when I had to do my chores when the neighborhood kids wanted me to come out and play. I remember having to clean the dishes after dinner. Out the window I would see a bunch of my friends running around playing tag or some other game. I wanted so much to be out there, but was not able to join them until the dishes were done. I loved to go out and play with my friends, but I would have to either wash or dry the dishes, trading off with my sister Colleen. Until the dishes were done, I wasn't going to get to say yes to the plea at the door from my friend Bob, "Can you come out and play?" I badly wanted to be outside hanging around and playing with my friends. Ninjas bring a whole new meaning to the phrase "hanging around." As a kid I could not have imagined the swinging and hanging around that I do on obstacles these days, as a ninja at my age. It's so fun to hang around at any age. I hope you're already hanging around. I loved to play and I still do.

At that time I had not figured out how to turn my cleaning-the-dishes chore into a game while I was waiting to get outside to play. I could have set a timer to see if I could beat my time to help keep me focused on my task. I could have changed the order in which I washed them to provide some variety and make it a little more fun. There are several things I could have done to turn that chore into a game, but I didn't.

Make It a Game

My dad used to occasionally cut our backyard grass in a curvy maze for us kids to play on. As an adult and homeowner, I now know why it was the backyard and not the front yard; I'm sure the neighbors appreciated a nicer-looking, well-cut front yard. It was so much

fun to run through the maze, jumping across the cut areas and sometimes playing tag where everyone had to stay in the cut area while they were being chased. That is a lifetime memory and one that shows how the simplest situation can be made into a game. That experience as a kid probably led to why I created Ninja Balance Obstacle Tag, which we sometimes play at MLAB OH during open gyms.

How are you turning your responsibilities into games or opportunities to play? If you're not, you should!

One of the tips I learned from one of the John Maxwell Team faculty members was to set a timer when I have to get something done. The task then becomes a game as I focus on what is in front of me, trying to beat the clock to complete the task and win the little time game I just created. It can be as simple as going through my emails and responding to them within 15 minutes, which sometimes can be a real push and a race against the clock.

Sometimes I find it best to bundle two or three activities together and give myself a time to complete all of them. It could be organizing the things I need to do for the day, calling someone, or outlining and writing a first draft of a writing assignment. I might give myself 35 minutes to complete these tasks, which is achievable if I stay focused. It becomes a game. Can I win? It's so much fun to beat that clock!

Using a timer helps me focus, and when I don't beat my time, I just reset the clock and start again, staying on my mission to see if I can get it done before my next alarm. I turn these activities into a game instead of just following through on a bunch of things I have to do. It enables me to have fun, stay motivated, and focus on the things that are most important.

Ninjas Love to Play

Ninjas play a lot and have a lot of fun when they have access to any space or objects on this planet, especially when they're around other ninjas. It can be in the hallway or bathroom of a building, in the entrance to a store, or on the steps to a school or church. It seems that any and every space is a place to see if we can do something new or better than we have before. I have adopted that orientation as well. I may not always take action on my thoughts, but boy do I have the thoughts! "I wonder if I could..."

Here are a few examples of what I've done to play over the past few years. After an Ohio State University (OSU) Buckeye basketball game, Carolyn and I were walking through the narrow, painted-cement-block hallway from inside the arena to the concession stand area. The hallway is wide enough for two people to pass comfortably or three to pass tightly. I couldn't help it. I saw that hallway as a ninja spider-jump op-portunity. I said to Carolyn, "I think I can stick this." I meant jumping up in the air, kicking my feet out, and sticking one foot on each side of the hallway, suspending my body in the air. I would not have tried it if the walls were drywall; I know that could have turned out badly, with a big hole in the wall.

With a grin I looked to Carolyn to see how she would react. She responded with, "Really? Are you sure you can do it and not hurt yourself?" I wasn't warmed up, I was wearing jeans, and I had old tennis shoes on, but I said, "I think I can."

I checked behind me to make sure no one was coming; I handed her my empty souvenir Buckeye cup; and here we go. With a swing of my arms and hands, I leaped into the air and kicked out my feet and... not quite. I slid down the concrete blocks. Okay, one more time, here we go. I swung my arms down and back and then up into the air in front of me, and pop, my feet kicked out, and... sure enough, my shoes stuck to the walls! This brought a gigantic smile to my face, ear to ear. My shoes were clean, so no marks were left on the wall. I checked.

It's so much fun to try something I've not done and make it, or at least come close. When I miss, my mind says, "What could I have done differently?" In this case, "I stuck it! I won!" on my second attempt.

Want to Try?

We are OSU Buckeye fans and we usually go to at least a game or two each year; basketball is my favorite team sport. One time we were at the arena and heading to our seats, and I needed to visit the rest room. Carolyn went on ahead. When I approached our section I saw Carolyn in the hall, holding her coat and watching something. It was a Marine Corps booth where you are challenged to see how many pull-ups you can do. She said, "I was guessing you were going to want to try to see how many pull-ups you could do." She was right; another chance to play.

A young marine had apparently completed seven pull-ups. A photographer for the game, a guy who said he was 63, saw me approaching the bar. I was in my jeans, with no warmup, and we had just eaten! The 63-year-old said, "Okay, I did nine. Can you do nine?"

I said, "We'll see." I stretched out my arms and got in place below the bar. They offered some pegs I could stand on to get to the bar, but hey, I'm a ninja. I have to jump up to the bar. I did so with a grin and a level of satisfaction, and here we go.

The dress shirt I was wearing came out of my pants as I pulled myself up to do a perfect pull-up, with full extension of my arms at the bottom. I've always been proud of my perfect pull-ups: full down, nice and slow, with full arm extension at the bottom, and then all the way back up again. This includes my chin fully above the top of the bar. (Unfortunately that pull-up technique does not help me with the salmon-ladder move, where you need more of a strong jerking motion.) My first five pull-ups went smoothly. The next one, two, three, and then four got a lot harder as that wings-and-fries dinner came very clearly to my mind. But I did it! I matched his nine, slowly. I still had some energy left. I had to push through. Slowly and perfectly, I was able to get my chin fully above the bar one, two, and finally three more times, for a total of 12 pull-ups! Those last couple of pull-ups were not pretty, but I did get them. That was cool. Wow, 12 pull-ups without a warmup.

When I came down, shook out my arms, and then posed for a picture or two, I remembered that my PR at the gym was 11 pull-ups and that I had not recently tried to beat that record. It was a spur of the moment PR, and in public. During one of the game time-outs a short video of my performance was displayed on the large screen. I was shown along with others who had tried the challenge. It's a lot of fun to play, at any age.

Like a Cliff-Hanger

I arrived early for a meeting at church. There are double glass doors at the entrance of the church, and I looked up and saw the solid metal frame supporting the propped-open door. I just hopped up, grabbed the two sides of the frame and did a few pull-ups, and then walked my hands from one side to the other, like a cliff-hanger on a ninja course. Ninjas just love to explore, have fun, and see what they can do.

Play Some More

I believe life is better when we include some time to play – and maybe a bunch of it. When we turn boring activities into games, they become enjoyable opportunities to challenge ourselves. It's play when we enjoy growing or performing beyond what we have done before. It can be something physically challenging or just doing something with our minds.

This play shows up for ninjas whenever they have access to any physical space, and especially at a ninja gym. Many gym owners open

their gyms the night before a competition so ninjas can come in and have fun. They get to see what they can jump to and from, run across, swing from, bounce to and from, push off, or any number of other moves. The next day, after the exertion and play of the night before, they line up to compete on the official ninja course. A competition can take anywhere from five to 12 hours.

What happens immediately after a competition? There is often another one, two, three, or even four hours of ninjas just hanging around playing and trying obstacles. Now that they have seen their peers take on obstacles in their own unique ways, there are new approaches and ways to try to beat the obstacles. They're hungry to get back out there and try more options. This time is called "redemption time," when you get to try again to beat an obstacle that may have taken you down during the formal competition. Ninjas also often try to see who can do the most of some new, unique thing. Who can last the longest on a dead hang? Who can do the most pull-ups? Who can bounce the highest on a trampoline (tramp) and grab and hold the highest obstacle? Who can... you name it. It's about play and challenging ourselves to achieve more than we have before. It's like one big round of King of the Hill.

Are you playing? What new ideas came to mind as you read my examples above? What can play look like for you? I'm convinced there are so many options for adding fun to our routine lives through adding the idea of playing.

Life is so much better when you're encouraged and supported and when you include play in your life.

Next we'll talk about how important it is to stay with it when you're working to accomplish something, and also how to face your fears.

Chapter 10

The Right Environment – Traits 7 and 8

7. Growth and Strength Take Time and Work

How quickly do you expect to see progress when you're working on an assignment or goal? Your goal might be developing a totally new skill like playing the piano (a middle-school experience for me); riding a unicycle (I also learned to do that in middle school); speaking a new language (like my attempts at Russian when Michelle was working in Kazakhstan); riding a two-wheeled wave board (which I learned in my fifties); giving engaging, powerful speeches (which I learned in my late fifties); or any number of other goals. You might want to bench press a certain weight, run a mile in a certain amount of time, or beat a specific computer game.

Growth and significant progress do not often come quickly. Regardless of your focus, in most cases making significant progress or developing a new skill or strength takes a long time of continual effort and practice. In most cases we have to achieve many small, even what might feel like tiny improvements over time, before we feel we have made progress.

Repeated Effort

Ninjas quickly learn that it takes time and repeated effort to achieve a new milestone on an obstacle or course. That's why they spend hour after hour, day after day focused on the same small element of a skill until they achieve the improvement they're looking for. Ninjas Noel Reyes and Bryce LaRoche shared with me how long it took them to master a slack line. Now it's amazing to watch them walk or do tricks on one. They make it look effortless because they dedicated significant time, focus, and effort to develop that balance skill and the muscles required to be on a slack line.

I could share many examples of me personally putting in that kind of time and effort, but probably the best example is the year and a half I worked on getting to the top of a 14-foot warped wall. That's running up the wall, grabbing the top, and pulling my chest above the top of the wall. At MLAB OH the ceiling interferes with standing on the top of the wall, so pulling my chest above the top was the goal to prove I had the strength to be able to stand on the top.

Two Hours... A Little Perspective

Michelle was able to reach and catch the top of the warped wall at Movement Lab New Jersey the first weekend she visited there! That wall is one of the hardest and steepest in the country. She worked specifically on wall attempts for over two hours before she stuck it for the first time. Many of the guys use a three-step approach to run up the wall, which she tried. Then she tried a four-step approach and almost got the top. Once she changed to the four-step  approach she soon caught the top. She is just five feet four inches tall. Your height makes a big difference. I don't know how many times she attempted the wall during that two-hour period, but if she attempted it three or four times every five minutes, she probably made 30 or 40 attempts an hour. From personal experience I can guarantee you each attempt drains you of energy and makes the next attempt that much harder. I need a good breather between attempts. Michelle really stuck with it until she reached her goal!

I was 57 when I started to attempt catching the top of a 14-foot warped wall. I spent more than 18 months and made over 1,000 attempts before I was able to reach and hold on to the top for the first time. I made at least 15 attempts most weeks for 18 months. I stayed focused and continually worked on my strength, technique, and

mindset, which are all so critical. That was a lot of work for a 57/58-year-old.

I finally reached that milestone in early 2016, just days before my 59th birthday. I had set a goal of getting it before I turned 59. Mission accomplished! Growth like that takes time and a lot of work.

Take the Hill

I've been calling the warped wall "a hill." I just keep running up the hill until I get to the top. When we first see a warped wall in person, standing on the floor and looking all the way to the top of it, I believe many, especially new ninjas, see it as a tall, hard, nearly straight up monster of a brick wall that is nearly impossible to climb, be it 12 feet, 14 feet, or higher. Seeing it as a hill that I'm running up instead of a wall helps me more easily visualize making it to the top.

There are guys at our gym who run up that wall with such power that they go for touching the building ceiling above the top of the wall, which is probably another three feet higher. This makes their top reach more like 17 feet. It's still baby steps for me with a 14-foot wall. My focus continues to be on getting better at consistently catching the top.

The warped wall is just one example of over 100 skills I've been working
on and slowly, consistently, and gradu-
ally making progress. Some of these
skills are leg strides, trampoline jumps,
ring swings, pegboard moves, laches,
and hops (a forward hop up with both
feet). I can now hop up 32 inches
(slightly less than three feet) seven
times in a row.

Earlier I discussed the term *yet*.
These are examples of applying *yet* in

my life. The key is celebrating each of my tiny improvements on each of these skills.

Pay the Price

Where are you frustrated with your progress? Where are you giving up when you should be pushing through? How much longer should you work at achieving your goal? How long is just too long? How much effort is too little, and you need to persevere and stay with it?

Progress and significant improvement require time and hard work, and a ninja is willing to pay that price. How about you? Are you willing to pay that price to gain that prize you have been working for? I hope you are.

Growth and progress feel so good and create so many new opportunities for us. They give us hope and energy, which spill into the other areas of our lives. You can grow and become so much more than you are today. I know you can!

8. Do It Even in the Midst of Fear

Where do you face fear? (We all do!) What fear is shutting you down or holding you back from achieving something that is important to you or could have a powerful impact on your life? Fear is a tremendously powerful issue for all of us. The more we learn to face it, embrace it, and overcome it, the better our lives become on all fronts.

You must do the thing which you think you cannot do.

– Eleanor Roosevelt

Ninja warrior is about facing your fears and overcoming them. From the day I stepped on my first ninja obstacle – the quad steps on

a late Saturday night at the end of one of Michelle's ninja competitions – to this day, I've been learning to better face fears, head on. I'm now bolder when facing many of my fears, though there are still those that shut me down.

Baby Steps

I've found that taking baby steps toward facing my fears is one of my best strategies. These include taking on my first eight-foot lache, the quad steps, my first salmon ladder rung, and so many others.

We used baby steps with under-five-feet-tall ninja Peggy Hale when she couldn't yet catch a 10-foot-high bar from a mini-tramp. We started by moving the tramp closer to the bar. As she experienced consistent success, we pulled the tramp back another five inches. We continued pulling the tramp farther back and she nailed it repeatedly, pulling the tramp back by baby steps until she had reached her maximum skill level for that day. It was a lot of fun to watch Peggy nail it from a much greater distance by first experiencing success from a short distance. Baby steps.

I used that same strategy for my growth on the very challenging MLAB OH cliff-hanger, which has only a one-and-a-half-inch ledge for your finger grip. I broke it down into mini-steps by working separately on my lateral swing move from hanging on the ledge and then also on my pull-up strength to the next higher cliff-hanger ledge. Once I was stronger and had better technique with each of these, I worked on the full swing, reach, and grab move to go across the whole cliff-hanger. Based on my experience I knew I would be much more successful because I broke each of these down into mini-steps. I've now been able to fully cross this difficult cliff-hanger. It feels so good to have another milestone achieved and a new PR.

In my first attempts on a salmon ladder I used the tip of simply jerking the bar up to the bottom of the next rung, which was a tremendous help. By doing that repeatedly without attempting to get over the next rung, I was able to practice the jerk move without having to focus on the pull out, reach up, and placement of the bar on the next rung. It's amazing how helpful these baby steps can be in learning how to beat an obstacle, or just one step of an obstacle.

Both large and small trampolines were foreign to me. I had not played on a tramp when I was growing up. I started my first real tramp experience at age 58, at MLAB OH. Many of my peers have hundreds or thousands of hours of a jump (pun intended) on me on the tramp. That being said, today I can't do many of the things they can do... yet.☺ So I'm taking baby steps on this intimidating and scary obstacle. During open gym times I often go to the tramp and just jump up and down, getting used to the feeling, the motions I need to take, and the results I get. In time I will become a lot better. The keys to overcoming these challenges are time and taking baby steps.

What fears do you face? Whether it's meeting new people, having a hard conversation with someone, learning a new subject, learning a new phone or computer – you name it, fear is common in all our lives. What baby steps can you take to help you move forward so you don't have to take on the whole challenge at once? How can baby steps help you experience some success and move you closer to facing your fear and addressing your challenge? Taking baby steps is a great strategy.

F.E.A.R.

Fear has been described as False Expectations Appearing Real – F.E.A.R. That's a pretty good description of fear for many of us. How true is this statement for you: I've experienced many horrible things in my life... most of which never happened (my version of a quote often mistakenly attributed to Mark Twain)? When we imagine the worst, our mind takes us through that experience as though we were living it, which makes us worry. When we view a situation ending in a good way, we gain the benefit of hopeful thinking even if it doesn't fully turn out that way.

I have found that by breaking my fears down into baby steps on ninja courses – little successes – I can face more fears than I have in the past. I have learned that many of my fears truly are just fears, that they are not real, and that they are just False Expectations Appearing Real. I can do more than I thought I could. Working with baby steps on a ninja course has improved other parts of my life as well. Writing books is one more example of overcoming fear. I'm now an author of four books and more are coming! I did it (with the encouragement and support of many others)!

What fears are holding you back? How can you better face them? What are some baby steps you can take? It feels so good inside when you're able to overcome a challenge. How could a gym or a ninja course be helpful to you in this way? It's an excellent place to practice overcoming fears. Why not give it a try? I'm convinced it can really help. And at a minimum you will experience something new, which is always exciting!

What type of environment do you live in? Being in a positive, encouraging environment makes a big difference in our lives. To be healthy and strong you need to be patient as you work at learning or accomplishing something, and you need to make sure you're not allowing fear to shut you down.

We're forced to study and learn when in school. In the next chapter we'll see how ninjas love to study and learn.

Study –
Traits 9 and 10

9. The Desire to Listen, Study, and Learn

Do you listen to, study, and learn from others when you're facing a tough challenge? Do you say, "I've got this"? There are so many things we can accomplish when we watch and learn from others.

Open Gym Times

Many gyms are open for two to four hours the night before a competition. This is a time for ninjas to see the gym and get to play on some obstacles, even though they will not see the actual obstacles that will be set up for the competition. These are fun nights, and in many ways even more valuable to me than the actual competitions.

I love these open gym times because I get to see how ninjas take on an obstacle that I've never seen or one that is set up differently than I've seen. There is so much to learn just by watching.

It's also an opportunity to study and personally try obstacles that are not in my home gym. The buzz around the gym on these evenings is "What do you think will be used for the course tomorrow?"  "What modifications will they make to the obstacles we see now?" "Will they eliminate a hold or a rope or extend the distance?" "What might they add that isn't currently set up?" "What have you heard that might surface in the morning at the comp?"

The buzz and evaluation are constant. We study how each obstacle is approached by each ninja, trying to figure out the best approach for us. "Can I reach the way he reached?" "Do I have the same finger strength or 90-degree hold strength that she has?" "Can his method work for me?" "What step, hold, or rope did she skip, and how did he accomplish that?" A lot of that study takes place the night before so that the ninja is ready to face the course the next day. The goal is to use everything you have learned in your training in the weeks and months beforehand so that you can be more efficient and effective in facing the obstacles back to back during a competition.

My Book-Writing Obstacle

The book-writing process, which I could look at as an obstacle, was something I had never done before. I could have just started writing and figured it out as I went, or observed, listened to, and learned from many others. I decided I could do it better and faster with the help of others who had already written books – those who were ahead of me.

I read three books on the book-writing process and then I joined a helpful group of writers. As they were writing their books, I asked questions, listened to, and learned from them, to help me take on my book-writing obstacle. I approached the process much differently than I would have if I had tried to do it on my own. And I was much more efficient and effective than I would have been without the help of these others.

I encourage you to listen to others and their ideas, and learn from their experiences, so you can be more effective in beating your obstacles. This way is so much better than taking the hard road by yourself.

Study is such an important element for growth. How would you be a better, stronger person if study were a bigger part of your life? What would change for you? We are not like trees that just need soil, sunlight, and water to grow. Make study a key part of your life.

10. Share of Yourself and Your Knowledge

Do you share what you know to help others? Do you give of yourself to help family, friends, or people you don't even know? The heart of a ninja is to provide encouragement and support to others and to also enjoy receiving it.

It's so much fun to help someone with something they are trying for the first time. It's rewarding to help someone go where they've never been. Most of us  get pretty excited when we achieve something new.

Sharing Tips

In my ninja experience there's a lot of sharing. The lache tips I received at MLAB OH from Jesse Wildman, Kyle Wheeler, and Josh Wallis were really helpful. I remember getting tips from 55-year-old ninja and gym owner Glenn Davis during the recording of *ANW* "All-Stars" in 2015. He shared with me various ways to grab a bar when swinging and lacheing. I'm reminded of tips I received from Jesse

Labreck on how to make a move on the BOSU® ball at the Rockford ninja warrior course. (A BOSU is a soft, two-foot-wide, half-round ball that tests your balance. The name BOSU comes from BOth Sides Up.) I appreciate the cannon-ball-swinging tips I received from ninja Sean Darling-Hammond, and the slack-line tips from Josh Wallis, Sean Noel, Noel Reyes, Bryce LeRoche, and others. I value the razor's-edge tips that Drew Drechsel shared with me after my 2017 run on the *ANW* city qualifier course. (I share much more about that in *What Just Happened?: The Run*, the story of my 2017 *ANW* course run in Cleveland.) I could go on and on with so many more examples.

These ninjas just wanted to help me get better at what I was trying to achieve. Often the advice is offered when I'm either attempting an obstacle or standing there studying it. Other times I just ask and the help is provided.

There is a wrong time to ask: just before a ninja is scheduled to run in a competition, or when they're already in a conversation with someone else. It's just common sense not to interrupt when someone is focused on what they're doing. I hope I'm getting better at asking only at good times. I know there have been times that I realized, after the fact, that I was making a comment or asking a question when someone was preparing to run the course, so now I'm careful to be sure I'm not interrupting their train of thought. And if you've asked and asked for advice and taken a lot of someone's time, let them get back to their own training. This is a very sharing community, and it goes both ways. Ninjas help each other and discuss approaches to obstacles all the time.

Where Could You Be Sharing?

What do you know that could be helpful to others? Who could be encouraged if you were to share with them something you know?

The key is to be sure that the person would like to know what you would like to share. We've all experienced being told something by a know-it-all. It's difficult to listen in those times, and easier when it comes from someone who we know cares about us. The best approach is to ask the question, "Would you like to hear my thoughts on how you could better do that?"

Ask for Help

The right insight or information can save you seconds (very important on a ninja course), minutes, hours, days, weeks, or even months or years. It takes both humility and boldness to ask someone for help. It can be scary to ask, but keep in mind that most people like to help, and if you don't ask you're taking away the opportunity for them to get to help you. The heart of a ninja is to share and receive a lot of what ninjas call "intel."

When we share of ourselves we become stronger. How can you learn and better apply this ninja trait?

In the next chapter I share how important it is to explore options when you're facing an obstacle, and also how important it is to learn to deal with failures. We all face them.

Chapter 12

Study –
Traits 11 and 12,
and a Summary

11. Explore Your Options

When you run into a prob-
lem or obstacle, how many
options do you consider? Often it seems we only identify
one or two options.

Many of us don't take the
time to look at an obstacle
from different angles, which
can prevent us from seeing
other ways to address it. We
feel trapped and limited in
how to face it. When we dread using the only option that comes to
mind, we try to avoid the obstacle altogether, which can make things
even worse.

When it comes to beating ninja obstacles, it's eye-opening to
watch the top ninjas. What appears to be a standard way to take on
an obstacle can be different from the way top ninjas do it. Yes,
there's a big gap between my skills and theirs, but I'm working to reduce the gap between the way I think about and approach an
obstacle and how they do it. I'm trying to take the time in advance to
think of at least three or four ways that I could approach an obstacle.

Ninja Options

I was competing in a mini-competition at MLAB OH. One of the early obstacles was a series of slanted steps set up in a unique way. There were seven slanted steps that formed an L shape.

I smoothly made it through the steps using a few single steps and a few triple steps. A little later one of the top ninjas who won the second competition that night, "The Ninja Mailman," Cory Cook, went through the same obstacle. He skipped one of the steps on the right because he noticed that the last three steps on the left were set much  like a ninja sonic curve, for which you single-step the steps as you round the curve to the end of the obstacle. This move feels more natural and it's a faster way to move through them. This technique could have saved me energy and two seconds on my run time. If you can save two or three seconds at five points along a course it reduces your time by 10 to 15 seconds, which can move you up the finish placement by several spots. That is significant in a competition.

Moving through a course with speed and efficiency is what wins competitions. Although ninjas always root for everyone to do their best, we want to do our best as well. When Carolyn and I were in the stands in 2015 at the first *Team Ninja Warrior* competition in Los Angeles, it was exciting to watch those talented ninjas go head to head focusing on efficiency and speed.

The fifth obstacle in that course was a set of two rings that you used to move along a number of pegs up and down a long inverted, V-shaped structure. It was very interesting to see ninjas use various

techniques to move across them as fast as they could. Some directly faced the peg and structure, a few had the strength and reach to skip a peg, and others used the rings more like monkey bars, swinging one hand down and under their body to swing forward to the next peg.

Then Drew Drechsel, a very talented ninja, was in a head-to-head match-up on the course. He was slightly behind when he got to the rings-and-pegs obstacle. When he got to the back third of that obstacle, he made one of his routine powerful swings backward, and the next thing we knew he was flying forward through the air toward the landing platform and past the other ninja. He skipped two pegs and flew forward over 15 feet – or rather SOARED! That move immediately put him in the lead and sent a chill of excitement through the entire crowd. To see him soar that far through the air was amazing! No previous competitor had attempted that move and taken that risk. Drew did it. He was the first. Soon others used the same technique, or at least tried it. Some were successful and some were not.

Drew thought it through, considered his options, and with his incredible strength and body awareness made a fantastic move that saved him energy for the end of the course. It also saved him valuable time and gave the crowd a tremendous experience to enjoy and savor.

Drew is one of my favorite ninjas. I love to watch him compete in the skills challenges that follow the *ANW* finals in Las Vegas. Watching Drew perform on the shelf-grabber/lache challenge is incredibly exciting. It's one of my favorite experiences. He can really SOAR!

Unlimited Options

Our options are almost unlimited if we take the time to think before we act. With preparation and dedication to developing body awareness, the most experienced ninjas can make adjustments in a split second. Sometimes what we envision will work goes wrong in the moment, and quick changes are required. Additional options on a course can include skipping a rung, step, or knob; single-stepping something instead of using multiple steps; reducing the number of steps used; building your swing before making a transition; using the swing of your body to assist you through a series of hand obstacles rather than using only your strength; using your feet on a rope or an I-beam to save your arm strength; leaning forward as you approach a warped wall; and so many others.

Great ninjas consider many options before taking on an obstacle. They leverage their abilities to maximize their performance. They use the options that will work best for them based on their current strengths and weaknesses.

How many options do you consider when you face a problem or obstacle? Do you consider your strengths and weaknesses? Sometimes it's hard to take the extra time, but it's worth every minute.

12. Failure Is Part of Growing and Getting Stronger

How does failure fit into your life and growth? If it does, does it move you toward growth and a greater commitment to learn, or

does it shut you down and send you into discouragement or depression?

Ninjas know that failure is a part of the process. Ninja courses and competitions are about learning to deal with disappointment, both on *ANW* and in local ninja competitions. Very few competitors successfully finish a course, and even when they do, it is rarely on the first try.

I have not failed. I've just found 10,000 ways that won't work.
— Thomas Edison

ANW City Qualifier Disappointment

One hundred to 110 ninjas typically get to compete on a city qualifier course. Of those, only 30 percent or less qualify for the finals. That means that 70 or more competitors will no longer be competing that season. That can create a lot of disappointment, and those ninjas whose season has come to an abrupt end could consider it a failure. This feeling of disappointment can be quite strong, especially considering the years of training and preparation they have invested. "I could have" and "I should have" conversations can dominate the thoughts of those who fall earlier than they had hoped, which is most ninjas. The best way to use these thoughts and feelings is as motivation for more training.

ANW City Finals Disappointment

Of the 30 or so ninjas who move on to the city finals, only the top 12 (potentially a couple more based on the "women competitors" rule that was put in place in *ANW 9*) move on to the "Las Vegas Finals." Any ninja who finishes the city finals course gets invited to compete in Las Vegas, but that's usually far fewer than 12 ninjas. So over half of the competitors are likely to be very disappointed. *ANW* is about striving to succeed and learning how to deal with disappointment and failure.

Local Ninja Gym Competition Disappointment

Even at local ninja gym and ninja league competitions, with between 40 and 100 competitors, sometimes only one ninja finishes the course, or only a few finish on a speed-based course, potentially five to 10 people. That is still a 70- to 95-percent failure or disappointment rate. This sport definitely requires you to learn to deal with disappointment.

How do I respond when I've failed on an obstacle? Do I get frustrated and yell at the obstacle? Do I blame the balance beam, the bar I swung from, or the step I slid off? Do I make excuses? Do I think, "I can't do this!"? Do I say, "I hate this stupid course!"? No. At least not for long. I respond like other ninjas. I say, "I can't believe I just did that. I should have... stepped out farther, reached higher, skipped that step, or whatever to make it through that obstacle," and then I get a very strong urge to get right back on that obstacle and try it again with a better approach. I think about my performance, watch a video of my run, and study what I did and didn't do well. I get tips from fellow ninjas, and then I get right back to work on trying to beat that obstacle.

As soon as I get home, I do what I can to duplicate the obstacle that took me out. I also set one up at the gym. (Remember, though, to have an adult check the safety of any obstacle you set up before you try it!) I want to practice and practice until I'm able to beat that obstacle that took me down. I know with a little more preparation and focus I can beat the obstacle the next time I face it. And through my training I gain confidence in my abilities.

BOSU Step-Down

One example is when I went down on a BOSU-ball transition step-down to a snake bridge in a Rockford ninja competition. I studied that obstacle and tried to figure out how to better approach it.

At home I have a BOSU ball in the basement, so I brought it up-stairs and set it on our dining room floor where there is a step down to our family room. It's only a six-inch step down, but when you add the height of the BOSU ball, it's a 13-inch drop, which was a perfect distance to practice. I practiced by bending one knee and extending the other foot in front and down the step to our family room floor.

As with my other obstacle experiences, my first few attempts were quite hard and not very successful. But the more attempts I made with each foot, the better I got at making that step. (I was tempted to use the word *easier*, but that is probably an overstate-ment of my skill; it is still a challenging move.) I set up a similar obstacle in our garage and practiced the move there as well. I also set up the BOSU ball in the basement as a part of a mini-course with sev-eral balance obstacles. In that setup I moved to the BOSU ball from a teeter-totter and then had to step down onto a large PVC pipe that rolls along the floor, a version of what many ninjas call a balance tank.

I set up a similar BOSU-ball obstacle at MLAB OH during an open gym. I was stepping down from a vault box that held the BOSU ball, making it a much farther step down to a handrail-like balance obstacle. This was a much tougher challenge than just stepping down to the floor.

When an obstacle beats us, we want to work hard on that skill to ensure to the best of our ability that the same obstacle will not take us out in the same way again.

Again, if you set up an obstacle on your own, be sure it is safe before you try it!

Only Four Feet

I fell on the third obstacle of a ninja course. I had to stand on a balance tank (PVC pipe) and roll it six feet across a rubber mat floor with my feet. I only made it four feet before falling. My response was the same as I shared in regard to the BOSU-ball experience. I now have multiple balance tanks at home and multiple carpets and mat floors to roll across. I'm now much better prepared for the next time I face that obstacle. I even keep a balance tank in my car trunk just in case an opportunity arises to play or entice other people to join me. I'm continually working to learn better ways to raise my skills.

*The definition of insanity is doing the same thing
over and over and expecting different results.*
— Albert Einstein

I love this quote that I heard over 20 years ago: "Any time the same dog bites the same person in the same place for a second time, it's time to blame... the person." Learn from your experiences – especially from your failures and mistakes.

Leadership guru, author, and speaker John Maxwell, in his book *Failing Forward*, wrote, "A lesson is repeated until it is learned." Every time I share this wisdom with a group, I say it slowly so that it can sink in for the listeners, and I often repeat it because I think it's so powerful.

Baby's First Steps

One of the best examples of this is how we support a baby when they attempt to take their first step. We don't yell at them for falling or failing. We don't tell them to give up or to believe they will never walk. Instead we celebrate every move they make toward taking that first step. We cheer them on. We help them in every way possible both physically and with our words.

Failure is a part of our learning process. We all need a community to encourage and support us when we fail, and the ninja community is an ideal family as we move through failure to success.

I do my best to live this way. I take time to think about my experiences so I can learn from my failures. I don't want to experience failure in the same way with the same result a second time. I'm not perfect in this area, but I've made great improvements.

How much better off would you be if you saw your failures in this positive way? It can make your life better. Where do you need to apply this type of thinking that failure is a part of growing and getting stronger?

12 Traits Summary

I have now introduced to you 12 traits of a ninja, grouped by obstacles, right environment, and study. Here is a brief summary of them:

Obstacles

1.   The desire to take on obstacles
2.   The desire to stretch and see how much you can grow
3.   It's you versus the obstacle, not others
4.   The knowledge that every obstacle is different

The Right Environment

5.   Encouragement, support, and celebration
6.   Always playing: everything is a game
7.   Growth and strength take time and work
8.   Do it even in the midst of fear

Study

9.   The desire to listen, study, and learn
10. Share of yourself and your knowledge
11. Explore your options
12. Failure is part of growing and getting stronger

I hope you're developing the heart of a ninja and that you're developing each of these traits in your life. I continue to work at better living each of these traits. I hope you found them helpful.

Now we're going to put into practice the concept of learning from others. What have you learned from your friends? How have they helped you improve your life? In the next chapter I share what I've learned from some of my ninja friends.

Chapter 13

Tips from Fellow Ninjas

What have you learned from others, especially those with more experience? What could you be learning from people who are older than you?

I've already introduced many of my ninja friends and shared about the encouraging relationships I've developed in just a few years. These are the people who support and motivate me. I reached out to a few of them to see if they would be interested in sharing their stories and everyone enthusiastically said yes. I asked them to share a little of their ninja training and experiences.

Everyone has a story. When we listen, we find out that everyone's story is interesting. I was in Christy Baldwin's SUV with five other ninjas on a long trip to Fort Wayne, Indiana, for a Classic City Ninja Warrior competition. To pass the time we took turns sharing short versions of our life stories. It was interesting and made the trip fun, and now I know them much better. You can learn something from everyone, and with most people it's as simple as asking a question and listening. In just that one trip I learned I was riding with two authors, a song writer, a chef, and a 12-sport athlete.

Each of the following ninja guests have done extraordinary things before and while they were becoming a ninja. Let's learn from their words of wisdom.

Dave Kozak

Sense of Satisfaction and Accomplishment

I enjoy physical challenges. As a kid I was tall, weak, and not a very good athlete. Now I enjoy physical activity. I enjoy meeting and exceeding personal goals and challenges. Something I can't do this week, maybe two weeks from now, if I work at it, I can. That gives me a great sense of satisfaction and accomplishment.

It's a Head Game

I have obstacles in my head that are bigger than the obstacles on the course. There are things that I know I can do if I apply myself, but I have to overcome this strong fear in my head. The greatest learning experience is that most of the obstacles we face, and there are the physical obstacles of course, are in our heads and are self-generated. That is the most important obstacle to overcome: our own thinking.

John Loobey

I don't have a gym close to me so my self-made gym at home includes a set of ascending steps on a hill. I also have a set of 10 flat steps. I have some pipes screwed to my swimming pool deck. I have a seesaw balance obstacle. I have a rolling PVC pipe. I have a knee-high rolling wire spool. I have a chin-up bar and some ledges that I use. I built a devil's ladder obstacle.

Prove It to Myself

I do ninja because it looks like fun and I enjoy doing it. I've been blessed with some health and strength and it is nice to put it to good use, proving to myself that I can do these things. I've always loved the show. I have watched it even when it was in Japan and only in Japanese.

Michael Moore

I met Michael in Las Vegas a couple of years ago. We were talking on the sideline about the performances and various ninjas of the night. It didn't take long to begin talking about our personal experiences. Michael shared some of his experiences and the things he had learned. Then he looked at me and asked, "Hey, when are you going

to get into this game?" I told him I had been thinking about it and that I had done some training, specifically my recent attempts on the warped wall. Michael smiled to indicate he knew that struggle and offered some advice. He told me that to get to the top of the warped wall you need to work on box jumps or hops, an exercise in which you stand on the ground and swing your arms and your body up, working to stick or stand on top of a box. I think Michael's challenge was to get to a 36-inch hop-up. "Do that," he said, "and you will have the strength to get to the top of the warped wall." It was helpful advice and it has paid off.

Michael shared that his greatest lesson is that he really could be more, do more, than what he thought he could. So can you!

Tips from Michael:

- Believe in yourself and know that you can do more than you're doing right now.
- It doesn't matter where you start or finish. It's about continuing to get a little bit better with each attempt.
- Work on balance. It's really important. Balance helps you in everything you do. It's surprising how balance can even help you do a better pull-up.

Selena Laniel

Walk Away Proud

What I've learned from ninja is that it's okay to fail. I know that sounds weird, but it was extremely hard for me to understand. It still is at times. To give it your all, to give it your best is what matters.

With ninja, that's exactly what you do every single time you set foot on that course. The outcome is the outcome. It eats you alive. You play it back in your head over and over. "What if I had done this? What if I had done it that way? I should have done this! Ugh." It's hard, but I've learned to accept the outcome and realize how lucky I am to take part in any of it! And if I can walk away feeling like I did all I could, to walk away proud of my accomplishments, proud to be there among some of the best athletes in the world and consider myself as one of them... I WIN!

Thanks to these Special Ninja Guests

These ninjas are each great examples of focusing on and experiencing personal growth. They have helped improve my ninja training and they have enhanced my life. I hope you're now also motivated to take your life to a new level. I share many more tips from these and additional ninjas in my first book, *The Heart of a Ninja*.

What friends are you learning from? We can learn so much from those around us.

Chapter 14

You, Too, Can Train
as a Ninja Warrior

I Won

Over the past few years I've developed the heart of a ninja. It has been an unbelievable experience. I won, and so can you by playing and moving, training as a ninja. I've been a typical non-athlete. If I can do this and love it, learn and grow, and have more fun and energy, you can too. All of us enjoy experiencing forward progress. You can improve your life, which will also positively impact your friends and family. It will make a difference. You matter!

Your Summary

Hopefully you have already made some positive changes based on what I've shared to encourage and challenge your heart and mind. I hope you will make even more changes in your life as you think about the key points from this book. Improvements you make in yourself benefit you for the rest of your life.

Your Next Steps

What would be an appropriate next step forward for you right now? There are so many things you can do to add movement and play to your life. Here are a few ideas:

Google Searches

Use Google (or any other browser) to explore ninja warrior on the internet. I list some good Google search options in the "Ninja Resources" section at the back of this book. There are also many helpful ninja-related YouTube videos.

At Home

- Start skipping a step as you climb steps at home. Start with skipping one step each time as you climb a flight of stairs. Then see if you can skip more than one. Finally, skip steps all the way to the top, or really push it and try skipping two steps. Make it a game. Set your own PRs to incorporate movement and play.

- See how far you can hop forward on a sidewalk or driveway, or if you can hop across a sidewalk. How far can you go the first time, and then how much farther can you go with additional attempts? Set a PR.

- Walk around the block. To turn it into a game, time yourself for a specific distance, trying to continually reduce your time; or set a time limit and see how far you can walk in that time, constantly trying to set a new PR — a greater  distance traveled within that time. Can you get to an additional mailbox or a few feet farther each time?

- Sit on the floor and do some stretching. Touch your elbows to your knees and see how many you can do or how long you can hold a position. Keep track of your PR and see if you can improve on it.

- See how many steps it takes you to travel a distance – maybe 20 feet or five sections of a sidewalk. Try to reduce the number of steps you have to take. How long of a stride can you use and still maintain your balance? Set a PR and improve on it. Have fun beating your own record.

- See how long or how far you can skip. It's a fun, playful, and freeing motion. Just doing it will bring a smile to your face. You can do it on a sidewalk, at the edge of a street, or in a parking lot. I usually try to do this either with others at a gym or when no one is around. That might apply for many of these fun suggestions.

At School

- See how many steps you can skip or how few steps you can take to the next floor or floors. Try doing it with no hands. You can even time yourself to see how fast you can do it.

- Stride from one colored tile or shape on the floor to another.

- Do a pull-up on a solid doorframe.

- Stretch while you're sitting or standing. How long can you hold it?

- See how long you can balance on one foot.

- See how many squats you can do.

- While standing on one leg, how many times can you bend over and touch the floor or something close to the floor? Remember, you have to do it with each leg. One may be a lot stronger than the other.
- See how many push-ups you can do.
- Find a tree outside your school that you can jump to, swing from, or do pull-ups on.

At a Park

- Climb up to and hang from the top support bar of a swing set or from a tree branch. How long can you hang? These are referred to as dead hangs. Try a pull-up, and if you're ambitious, try shaking out,  which is when you hang by one hand and let the other arm dangle while you shake it out. The first time you do this will give you a quick sense of just how hard it is. It will help you appreciate what other ninjas can do.
- Balance on one of those concrete parking barriers at the front of a parking space. (Use one that does not have a car parked in front of it!☺) How long can you stay on? If you

really want to have fun, try stepping across them from one parking spot to another. Those can be quite long strides and they are fun to try.

At a Ninja Gym

- Find out when a local ninja competition is taking place and go watch it.
- If you're within traveling distance of Columbus, Ohio, enroll in a Ninja Lite class at MLAB OH and learn from me as your instructor. I focus on safety, fun, and beginner ninja skills, in that order!
- Go to an open gym time at a ninja gym and start with a few simple obstacles.
- Set up or ask an adult ninja to help you set up a mini-course during an open gym time. Start with just three or four obstacles that focus on balance. Time yourself and see if you can make it through without falling from any of the obstacles. Just focus on improvements: fewer falls or less time to complete the mini-course. If you want to get creative, change the obstacles to make them just a little harder to complete.

- Enter a local competition. Many gyms offer various levels of competition. You don't have to start at the pro level. Enter the amateur, basic, or lowest level of competition. MLAB OH even offers what they call mini-comps for just a few dollars and a few hours – not a full-scale, all-day event.

I hope these ideas open your mind to the unlimited number of ways you can include movement and play in your life, wherever you are. You can do it, and it will be good for you.

Thank you!

You have finished *The Heart of a Ninja for Kids*. Thank you for joining me on this journey. I hope you enjoyed the experience and that you have learned some things that will help you. There are additional ninja resources in the remaining pages.

Share This Book with Others

Pass *The Heart of a Ninja for Kids* on to someone you think would really enjoy it. You might want to recommend it to others or buy a copy for them as a gift. *The Heart of a Ninja for Kids* is a great birthday gift! If you would like others to know how much you enjoyed the book, please provide a review at Amazon.com.

Thanks for investing in yourself by reading this book. It will pay off for you. It's play time! Now get out there and live like a ninja!

Make it another great day, week, month, and year.

Your ninja, friend, author, coach, and *ANW* fan,

Chris Warnky

Afterword

In 2017 I made the decision to join the *ANW* Cleveland walk-on line. That was a wild and crazy experience that took place over a 16-day period. This experience resulted in my meeting many new friends and going through a bunch of new experiences. Read all about it in *What Just Happened?: The Line*.

On May 8th of that year I competed on the *ANW* Cleveland course. It was a blast! I take you along with me as I relive that wild and crazy experience in *What Just Happened?: The Run*. I share the process, challenges, and all the emotion about that amazing experience.

Ninja Resources

Ninja Gyms

Most gyms provide classes, open gym times, and competitions.

Movement Lab Ohio: http://www.mlabohio.com
　　　　email: Info@mlabohio.com

Movement Lab (New Jersey): http://www.mlabnj.com

Movement Lab (Los Angeles): http://www.mlabca.com

There are many new gyms opening all the time. The leagues below provide lists of gyms that participate in their leagues.

Ninja Leagues

National Ninja League (NNL):
http://www.nationalninja.com

United Ninja Athletic Association (UNAA):

http://www.ultimateninja.net

Athlete Warrior Games:

https://www.athletewarriorgames.com

Google Searches (content changes all the time)

- Ninja
- Ninja warrior
- Ninja gyms
- Ninja training
- Ninja camps
- Ninja leagues
- Parkour gyms
- Wolfpack tour

Equipment and Shoe Vendor Options

- 3Ball Climbing – cannon balls, etc.
- Atomik – cannon balls, etc.
- New Balance Shoes – Fresh Foam Zante (I use these for all my training. They're my favorites, with unbelievable traction for warped walls, spider climbs, etc.)

American Ninja Warrior News Site

- ANWNation.com

Learn More

Contact Information

Chris Warnky, author, ninja competitor, executive and life coach, motivational speaker, trainer, and owner of Well Done Life LLC

Cell phone: 614.787.8591 (call or text)

Email: chriswarnky@gmail.com

Facebook: welldonelife

Website: welldone-life.com

Blog: http://cwarnky.wordpress.com

Training as a Ninja

Attend a Ninja Lite session at Movement Lab Ohio with instructor Chris Warnky.

Ask about personal and individualized one-on-one Ninja Lite training sessions with instructor Chris Warnky.

Want Chris to Speak to Your Group?

Chris is available to speak to groups on a variety of topics including:

- Topics in his books
- Personal refocus times (retreats)
- Leadership and communication topics
- John Maxwell Team leadership materials

Upcoming Books

Chris has a number of additional books currently in the works.

Thirteen percent of initial profits from sales of Chris's books is donated to Mission Aviation Fellowship (MAF), and subsequent profits to MAF and additional charities.

Free Gifts

If you would like to receive any of the following free gifts, please request them at chriswarnky@gmail.com:

- A short video greeting from Chris with a bonus ninja training experience story
- A bonus story about Chris's 2017 NNL announcing experience

Be Mentored by Chris Using the 12 Traits of a Ninja

Chris offers "Twelve Trait Mentoring" (from his book *The Heart of a Ninja*), which has been especially ideal for young people who love *American Ninja Warrior* and can benefit from a strong male presence in their lives. Sessions can be conducted in person, by phone, or via Facetime. Choose from 30-, 45-, and 60-minute sessions.

Be Coached by Chris

Chris provides both life coaching and executive coaching.

Acknowledgments

I'm thankful to our Creator/God for allowing me to live my first 62 years and for providing me with many great relationships and experiences. I'm also thankful to have peace with Him because of the life and sacrifice of His Son, Jesus.

Thanks, Carolyn, my wife, for your support during the time I have invested in writing, editing, and publishing this and other books. You are my love. I can't imagine going through anything without you by my side to celebrate our successes and support me in my times of failure and disappointment. I love you!

There are so many others I'm thankful to because of their contributions to my life and/or for their specific help with the writing, editing, and feedback on this book. Below are a few of them:

Thanks to my mom and dad for all the love and support you provided to me throughout my life. Thanks to Tim and Bonnie for your love and support. Thanks to Michelle for continually supporting me during my ninja journey.

Thanks to my Lunch Time Training Partners (LTTPs), Shanon Paglieri, Katie Tennant, Scott Walberry, Shea Stammen, Chad Kohler, and Rex Alba, who support me as we train and compete together. Thanks also to so many other MLAB OH ninjas I train with. I love spending time with you all.

I'm very thankful for all the great support and instruction provided by the MLAB OH instructors, especially those who have been there for so many open gyms and ninja classes. These include head instructors Jesse Wildman, Kyle Wheeler, Justin Allen, Drake Stevens, and Sophia Oster. You add so much value to the training for me and others. I appreciate you.

Thanks to the many ninjas across the country who have welcomed me and embraced me into your community. Thank you for the encouragement, support, and friendship, and the tips you've provided to make me a better ninja. I appreciate you.

A special thanks to the following parents for allowing me to share photos of their ninja kids: Francie and Nick Buschur for photos of their son Noah; Christina and Ken Yee for photos of their daughter and son, Sydney and Dylan; and Lauren Finkelstein for photos of her son Rafi Ellison.

Thanks to Gwen Hoffnagle, my professional editor for my first three ninja books. You have taken my original manuscripts to new and much higher levels. I enjoy working with you and appreciate the value you provide. I would recommend you to any author. Thank you so much! I really appreciate you.

About the Author

 Chris Warnky is 62 years young and has been married to Carolyn May Warnky for over 40 years. He has two children: Tim, who lives in Cleveland with his wife, Bonnie, and two daughters; and Michelle, who lives in Columbus and is a popular multi-year *American Ninja Warrior* competitor and a serious, competitive obstacle-course racer.

Chris is an active, training ninja warrior dedicated to his Lunch Time Training Partners. He is also an MLAB OH Ninja Lite instructor and offers personal one-on-one ninja-lite-level targeted training sessions.

He competed in the 2017 *American Ninja Warrior Cleveland City Qualifier* and has competed in numerous ninja competitions over the past couple of years including both National Ninja League and Ultimate Ninja Athlete Association competitions. He provided the play-by-play for numerous Facebook Livestream ninja competitions, including the NNL finals.

Chris has been a Bible-reading Christian for over 50 years. His relationship with God is the basis for his life.

He is an author with plans to write several additional books, a professional executive and life coach, and a thought-provoking speaker through his business, Well Done Life. He coaches clients addressing important life and business topics.

Chris is a certified coach, speaker, and trainer with the John Maxwell Team. He served two years on the organization's President's Advisory Council. He served two terms as the International Coach Federation Columbus Charter Chapter president. He achieved the Toastmasters International "Competent Communicator" designation.

Chris has over three decades of corporate leadership experience, including 23 years as a vice president at Bank One/JP Morgan Chase contributing as a project manager, program manager, and compensation manager.

Made in the USA
Coppell, TX
14 February 2020